THE
RING
IN THE
RUBBLE

THE RING

IN THE

RUBBLE

Dig Through Change and Find
Your Next Golden Opportunity

GARY BRADT

McGraw-Hill

New York   Chicago   San Francisco
Lisbon   London   Madrid   Mexico City
Milan   New Delhi   San Juan   Seoul
Singapore   Sydney   Toronto

The **McGraw·Hill** Companies

1 2 3 4 5 6 7 8 9 0   DOC/DOC   0 9 8 7

ISBN-13: 978-0-07-148851-8
ISBN-10: 0-07-148851-0

McGraw-Hill books are available at special discounts to use as premiums and sales promotions, or for use in corporate training programs. For more information, please write to the Director of Special Sales, Professional Publishing, McGraw-Hill, Two Penn Plaza, New York, NY 10121-2298. Or contact your local bookstore.

Library of Congress Cataloging-in-Publication Data

Bradt, Gary.
    The ring in the rubble / by Gary Bradt.
        p. cm.
    ISBN 0-07-148851-0 (alk. paper)
    1. Success in business. 2. Opportunity. 3. Diligence. I. Title.

    HF5386.B76 2007
    650.1—dc22   2007000672

To Peggy,
my enduring "Golden Ring" of hope,
love, and inspiration

CONTENTS

ACKNOWLEDGMENTS

A book is a creative stew, a melting pot of ideas stimulated by others and mixed together by an author-chef who strives to blend the ingredients into an appealing dish that he hopes will be appetizing and tasty to the reader's palate.

I want to thank those who have blessed me by providing the ingredients for the current dish. To the degree that it proves nourishing and satisfying, they deserve all the credit. Some have blessed me with friendship, some with love, all with their gift of wisdom and encouragement. So many thanks go to them.

To Fred Abbey, for seeing in me what I couldn't see in myself and helping me to unlock it; to Spencer Johnson, who generously took me under his wing and showed me how words can make the world a better place; to Ken and Thelma Bradt: nobody could ask for better parents or receive more complete and unconditional love and support; to Peggy Bradt, a lifeline whose beautiful countenance and presence sustains and serves me always; to Tony D'Amelio and Christine Farrell, who reviewed early versions of the manuscript and spurred me on; to Mark French and his colleagues, who have supported me from day one; to my agent, Lynn Johnston, for her unwavering guidance, advice, and advocacy; to my editor, Jeanne Glasser, for taking my words and making them better; to my most Precious Gems of all, Carson and Kimberly; and to all of my business consulting and speaking clients, who have entrusted me with their faith and allowed me to glimpse and share in the struggle and glory of their businesses and their lives. I am indebted to all of you for your contributions to this book.

THE

RING

IN THE

RUBBLE

MY STORY

The doctor's words hung in the air.

"As you know, your son is deathly ill. I am sorry to have to tell you that he could die at any minute."

When my two-day-old son was transferred to a teaching hospital, I knew that the situation was dire. It was Christmas Eve, 1988—the worst Christmas of my life.

The doctor continued.

"We know it's something with the heart, but we don't know exactly what's wrong. I have my best cardiologist on her way in. We'll do the best we can."

I stumbled to the nearest waiting room, where snippets of conversations with other doctors over the last few days flashed through my hazy mind: *premature birth . . . incubator . . . holes in the heart . . . misplaced aorta . . . low oxygen . . . don't know all that's wrong . . . we'll need to transfer to another hospital . . . ambulance . . . we'll do our best.*

It was a nightmare, but there was no waking up from this one. I sat stunned in the waiting room, inert. My firstborn was down the hall fighting for his life. My wife was back at the original hospital, held captive by medics who were concerned about serious complications she had suffered during delivery. Thankfully, her illness was not life-threatening.

I was a mass of confusion—alone, mad, and scared. I didn't know what to do or how to react to this sudden and unforeseen change. Our family's carefully made plans had been cruelly and dramatically altered. My life seemed to be crumbling around me—as if my hopes and dreams for being a father had been reduced to nothing more than a pile of rubble, an unsettling mixture of disruption, fear, and uncertainty. At the time, there was no way for me to know that within the rubble lay the opportunity for something better than I had had before my son's birth—and certainly better than I could foresee at that moment: a golden ring. Incredibly, out of this dark time came personal and professional enlightenment that I never could have foreseen.

Today, my son is 18, but his battle to live and the hardships my family endured over the next few years started an incredible journey of discovery that continues to this day. I have learned that change, while sometimes painful and difficult, always creates opportunities—the trick is to find them. These experiences have taught me guiding principles for uncovering the golden ring—the opportunities that lie within every situation and are created by change.

Many of you are wrestling with or will face unforeseen and unwanted change at work and at home. Others feel a gnawing need to make a change because standing still is no longer an option. My intention is to offer guidance and practical suggestions on how best to lead yourself and your organization through change; to help those who are looking for inspiration and motivation to carry on after having experienced a devastating change; and to provide insight and advice born from both my own experiences and others' to show you how to unearth that golden ring.

May you enjoy and benefit from the journey as I have.

INTRODUCTION

In business, we tend to take the simple and make it complex, and we take the complex and make it nigh on impossible. Consider the following scenario. A CEO pulls her team into a conference room and says:

> "Folks, government regulations, shifting technologies, industry consolidation, and geopolitical uncertainties have reduced our best-laid business plans to rubble. However, my experience says that buried within the rubble is a golden ring of opportunity. Finding it will catapult us far ahead of our competition. I believe it's our job as leaders and as an organization to find that ring. So, how do you recommend we proceed?"

I don't know what your experience has been, but many of the management teams I've observed over the years would probably come back with something like this:

> "Let's benchmark organizations that have successfully dug for rings before and develop a list of competencies. Then we can design a training program around that and put everyone through it."

"The union will never go for that. Digging for rings isn't covered under the current CBA."

"Even if it was, ring digging clearly is not in the budget. We simply can't afford it."

"Let's put together a blue ribbon committee of our high-potential people and let them come back with recommendations on what we should do."

The beleaguered CEO looks over at the corner where Jackson, the summer intern, is sitting quietly but attentively.

"Jackson, you've heard the situation we face. What do you think we should do to find the ring in the rubble?"

Jackson squirms nervously in his seat. His answer seems so obvious that he's embarrassed to say it.

"Well," Jackson says hesitantly, "if there *is* a ring in the rubble, why don't we just start digging?"

The earlier responses make good use of our metaphor, and while they are not inherently wrong, they do miss the point—except for Jackson's. How you handle change, personally and professionally, defines the line between winning and losing. Change is the great equalizer; it affects all of us. *Organizations that view change as an opportunity and aggressively seek to find and capitalize on it, win. Those that don't fall behind and are doomed to forever play catch-up.*

This applies to your personal life as well. Whether you're facing a new marriage, divorce, birth, death, or illness, it's not the change itself that dictates the results we get, it's how we perceive and handle that change that makes all the difference. This is the underlying premise of *The Ring in the Rubble*.

The ring represents the valuable opportunities that change always creates. The rubble symbolizes the disruption, fear, and uncertainty that change almost always stirs up. My goal is to help you find the rings in the rubble of whatever changes you face, both at work and at home.

More than that, I want to help you make change happen when standing still is not an option. Sometimes it's not change but the fear of *making* a change that holds us back. Have you known people who have stayed in jobs that they can't stand but won't leave because of fear of the unknown? Have you ever conceived of a brilliant plan at work but were afraid to implement it because of fear of failure? How many of us are stuck in broken relationships personally and professionally, but are unwilling to change ourselves to improve them?

The motivation for writing this book came from my many years as a keynote speaker on change management. The request I got from my sponsors and my audience was and remains the same, and that was to help people to see the opportunity in change—to embrace it. Before we begin, let me suggest a few things that will help you glean the most from your reading. The goal here is to help you think about the changes in your life and deliver ways in which you can get tangible results.

Take a moment right now to reflect on a change that is troubling you, one that has you confused as to where to turn or what to do. Professionally, maybe you've just lost your job or fear that you soon will. It's not unusual these days for someone to be downsized or right-sized or outsourced out of a job several times. Maybe you want to make a change—perhaps move to a different department, or even change careers or start your own business. If you're an executive, perhaps government regulations have your industry in a down cycle, or you're trying to figure out how to keep up with shifting technologies without breaking the bank.

At home, perhaps your marriage is in trouble or you're an empty nester for the first time. Or, you were an empty nester, but this year they came back! Maybe you or a loved one is fighting a serious disease, or you've recently lost a beloved friend or family member. Or, on the less serious side, maybe you just haven't reconciled yourself to the gray hairs looking back at you in the mirror.

Whatever your situation, I want you to think about it right now and notice how it makes you feel. Are you angry? Excited? Scared? Frustrated? Keeping this situation in mind will help you apply what you read as I help you search for the ring of opportunity that change represents. I can help you in your journey, but I can't tell you what your ring will look like. Each person has to define and identify his or her exclusive opportunity. I can't tell you exactly where you will find your ring, either, but I *can* assure you that it's there and offer guidelines that will help you discover it.

Having a variety of tools—shovels, picks, hoes, etc.—would come in quite handy when digging through an actual pile of rubble. So too, when digging through the rubble of change. Thus, you'll find that each chapter will provide a different guideline or tool for finding the unique opportunity that change has created for you, along with stories of individuals who have used each tool to their advantage so that you can see how you might put the tools into action. Each chapter will conclude with a series of questions designed to help you dig a little deeper into how this particular tool might apply specifically to you and help you deal with your unique change situation.

If you are part of a work team, you and the other team members may want to read the book together and answer the questions as they relate to your team or organization in an ongoing group discussion or team-building event. You may want to do the same thing in your personal relationships. Read a chapter each day and share your impressions and feelings with each other before you go to sleep at night. Or, you may want to read the book alone and privately reflect on its message.

However you choose to proceed, my goal is to help you find the possibilities that change always creates. I fervently believe that there is always a ring in the rubble and treasure in our trouble, no matter how difficult or painful the change may be.

But you would never have convinced me of that when our first child was born. In fact, it seemed quite the opposite. He was born deathly ill with a multitude of medical problems, a malfunctioning heart topping the list. This terrifying and unanticipated event threatened to ruin the life my wife and I had built together. In fact, it ultimately brought us closer, but the journey was often frightening and unpredictable. It was during this time that I discovered many of the principles for seeking out the opportunity in change that I share in this book. Thus, each chapter begins with another step in this journey, tracking the steps of my child's battle to survive. My hope and prayer is that this book will become a source of inspiration and enlightenment for you, and that your life will be enriched by whatever changes you may encounter.

Chapter One

YOU'LL NEVER FIND THE RING IF YOU DON'T START DIGGING

The answer came to me like a beam of light emanating from the rubble of fear and confusion: I'm a dad, and I may have this opportunity for only a very short time. Why am I wasting this experience by feeling sorry for myself? I cannot change the fact that my son has been born with these problems. I cannot control whether he lives or dies, but I do have power over what I choose to do next.

When unexpected change hits and turns the best-laid plans to rubble, it's normal to feel angry, scared, or confused, or perhaps a bit of all three. In fact, you should expect that.

It's like heading out the door for your drive home from work when someone suddenly informs you that all the traffic laws have changed: red no longer means stop, green no longer means go, and yellow no longer means *gorealfast*. Which side of the road to drive on, the street signs, and the traffic signals have all changed, but the new laws have yet to be written, and no one has a clue about what to do.

Can you imagine how disruptive that would be and how it would make you feel? Whenever things suddenly and dramatically change, fear and uncertainty are the norm, and sometimes anger too. The question, just like the one our mythical CEO posed to her team in the Introduction, is, what are you going to do next? Because *it is the actions you take that determine the outcome you get*. And your actions are determined by how you choose to view and think about the situation. *To change your actions, change your thoughts.*

If you let fear or anger control your actions whenever things change, you won't be successful because these emotions drive you into survival mode. And when you're in survival mode, you get desperate, and you do desperate things. Desperation rarely leads to the ring. You're much better off acknowledging the rubble and then deciding how to go about digging. Think of these emotions as nothing more than energy that you can put to better use. An amazing tale of survival demonstrates the point.

Richard was the owner of a successful chain of high-end electronics stores in the upper Midwestern United States. The stores were profitable and doing well. Then, within a matter of minutes, he nearly lost it all. In fact, much of Richard's business was literally reduced to rubble.

Suddenly, and with hellish ferocity, a tornado tore through his town, damaging Richard's largest and most profitable store, along with his warehouses and much of his inventory.

Richard's stores, his dreams, and the fruits of his labor were all suddenly in jeopardy. As so often happens, swift change had brought with it sudden and serious troubles.

Although I imagine that Richard was initially frightened and uncertain of his next steps, he didn't focus solely on the rubble by bemoaning his bad luck, bracing for a fight with his insurance company, withdrawing into himself, obsessively making plans, or simply giving up.

These were not productive thoughts or actions, and they would not lead to the ring. So instead, Richard started *digging*, taking bold and resolute action in the face of change and uncertainty. He decided to have a tornado sale, repairing the damaged inventory as well as possible, then opening the remaining stores and warehouses to the public and letting people pick items right off the shelves. Richard then used the company's advertising budget for the remainder of the year to spread the word: "High-end electronics at a discount!"

The strategy worked. On the day of the sale, people were literally lining up to walk through Richard's warehouses to pick up and buy his discounted items. It was his chain's most successful sale ever.

Richard had found his ring, but he didn't stop digging. Analyzing why the sale had been so successful, he came to realize that while his old business model of selling high-end goods at a high price through traditional stores was a good one, this new model of selling valuable goods at a discount using a warehouse model promised to be even better. After the ravages of the tornado, Richard decided to adopt this new approach permanently.

Before the tornado, Richard's chain had had nine or ten stores. However, because Richard and his people kept digging through the rubble of change, their treasures have multiplied dramatically. Today, the chain has well over 900 stores. Perhaps you've shopped there. Richard changed the name of his chain to Best Buy. Today, Best Buy is one of the most successful discount retailers of electronic goods in the world, and it got its start when its founder, Richard Schulze, was nearly wiped out by a tornado.

This story illustrates several guideposts for locating the ring within the rubble. First, you'll never find the ring if you don't start digging. Or, as Thomas Edison said, "Opportunity is missed by most people because it is dressed in overalls and looks like work." Second, you have to start digging even if you're not sure what the ring looks like and don't know exactly where it's hidden. You have to believe that it's there and take bold and resolute action, without getting bogged down in artificial busyness or, worse, sulking into inactivity. Training, planning, strategizing, and all the other things suggested in the Introduction have their time and place. However, if you are going to win when things change, you have to be willing to undertake meaningful, bold action. Third, it is important to understand that there is no guarantee that you'll find the ring right away. Sometimes your efforts won't be as successful as Richard's; you'll come up empty, or achieving your goal will take much longer than you had hoped. We'll deal with those scenarios in later chapters.

However, I *can* guarantee that if you do nothing, you will never find the ring. You will never reap the rewards and opportunities that are your due, and from a business perspective, you'll leave the benefits of discovery to your competitors, with your organization playing an eternal game of catch-up—hardly a winning strategy. Sometimes it's hard to get started. Our doubts or our fears keep us from digging. To get started, manage the way you think about your situation, because your thoughts will dictate your actions. Or, as I like to say, "Where you think, there you are." Are your thoughts leading you to act, or are they keeping you in suspended animation? Those who are the best at leading change possess a positive attitude that drives them toward action.

Chung Ju Yung, founder of Hyundai Corporation, rose from extreme poverty to head one of the largest and most successful businesses in the world. Time and again his company searched for new rings by expanding the scope of its products and services well beyond its traditional comfort zone. Ingvar Kamprad, the founder of the IKEA furniture chain, started out by buying goods like matches, vegetable seeds, and ink pens and reselling them to his neighbors in the tiny village where he lived. From these humble beginnings, he built IKEA into an internationally renowned industry leader. All three of these men—Schulze, Ju Yung, and Kamprad—shared a common trait: *they believed that they could succeed, and their beliefs led to positive action.* How often do we stop ourselves from digging for the ring of opportunity because we don't believe we can find it? We stop ourselves from trying before we ever begin.

You'll never find the ring if you don't start digging, and you'll never start digging if you don't believe in the *possibility* of success. In *Made in Korea: Chung Ju Yung and the Rise of Hyundai*, author Richard M. Steers quotes Chung: "Some men live without thinking. Other men with positive thinking achieve ten or one hundred times as much as ordinary people." This simple dictum, believing that you can succeed, is the first and primary tool to take with you on each and every dig you undertake. Without it, you're not likely to find the ring of opportunity other than through plain dumb luck. It's better to improve your odds by telling yourself *I can do this* whenever you are given the task of working your way through change or making change happen. Inculcating this positive mindset in yourself and others is step one toward finding the ring.

DIG A LITTLE DEEPER

1. *What plans of yours have recently been turned to rubble by sudden and unforeseen change?*

2. *Up until now, what have you been thinking and feeling about this change, and what actions have you taken?*

3. *Are your current thoughts and actions likely to uncover the ring of opportunity in the rubble?*

4. *If not, how can you change your point of view toward the situation to one that will lead you to take more fruitful action? Focus on what you can do, not on what you can't.*

5. *If you are having trouble getting started with your dig, what's holding you back? Fear? Anger? Lack of resources? A negative attitude? Whom can you talk to and what can you do to begin addressing these concerns? Remember, change your thoughts to change your actions.*

Chapter Two

LET GO

First, I prayed. I didn't know how long I was going to have my son—whether it would be five minutes, five hours, or five years—but I vowed that for as long as I did, I would love him with all my heart and soul. Beyond that, I accepted God's will. Second, I took decisive action, choosing to be near the team of doctors frantically ministering to my son. I wasn't going to leave him isolated from those who loved him. Yes, I was afraid and angry, but I chose to let those feelings go and focus on my love for my son. I changed my thoughts from "This is the worst Christmas ever" to "This is the best Christmas ever. I have a son." Doing these things helped me find a measure of peace, a ring amidst the rubble.

I magine that you have two sacks on the floor in front of you. One of them is labeled "If Only: Resentments and Regrets from the Past"; the other, "What If? Fears and Worries about the Future." Now, imagine filling up the If Only sack with all the things you remember from your past that stir up anger or regret. Take some time to really get into this. Make a mental list or grab a pen or pencil and write down whatever comes to mind. What would you put in your sack of Resentments and Regrets? Potential items may include memories of an abusive boss or coworker, or even a parent. Maybe events concerning an ex-spouse (or two!) come to mind. Or even that jerk who cut you off in traffic this morning. Into the sack they all go.

Now take a moment to reflect on all the things that haven't happened yet, but that you are worried about. They go in the What If sack. They may be big things, like fears of another terrorist attack on home soil and how such an event would affect your business specifically and the global economy in general, not to mention the implied human loss and suffering. Maybe you have an important presentation coming up that you are worried about, or a difficult performance review that you're not looking forward to conducting (or receiving). Maybe there's something minor but still worrisome, like travel plans that could be affected by the weather. You've bookmarked weather.com on your computer, and you constantly search for updates, expecting the worst.

Take your time. Be honest. What would go in your two sacks?

Now imagine picking up one sack and then the other one and flinging both of them over your back. From here on, you will take them with you wherever you go. You get up to go to the kitchen in the middle of the night? The sacks go with you. When you walk in for a job interview, the sacks and their contents are in tow. Calling on an important customer? The baggage calls, too. Asking someone for a date as you reenter the dating scene? Make room for your sacks (and those of your date). All of us carry sacks just like these with us all the time. For some of us, the sacks are lightly packed; for many, they are quite heavy. Some of us are *professional collectors*. Your boss walks by without saying good morning? You perceive that you were screwed out of a promotion? Into the sack. Your golf shot goes in the water? Splash. Anger. And then *plop*— into the sack.

Ironically, we put items into our sacks all the time, but we rarely, if ever, examine the contents of these sacks and throw stuff out, much less refuse to add to them in the first place. No wonder so many of us are constantly tired. The continual load gets heavy and saps our strength. The more we carry around resentments from our past and worries about the future, the less energy we have to notice and grab onto the opportunities of the present. We lack the capacity. We are too consumed by what has happened already or too worried about what might happen next to notice the opportunity that is staring us in the face right now.

When change presents a golden ring of opportunity we can't grab it because we are too busy clutching our sacks. Let me share with you a story that depicts what holding onto these sacks looks like and how it can affect your work life. See if this sounds familiar.

I was asked by a manufacturing CEO to sit in on his monthly management meeting. He complained that the group was failing to make progress. "Every month we meet as a team to gauge our progress toward our goals," he said, "but we seem to be stuck in neutral or going backwards. Maybe you'll see something we're missing that will help us move forward."

Did I ever. Tell me if you've ever sat in on this particular brand of meeting. I've come to call them "What's in Your Sack Meetings." All the vice presidents and division heads had to stand before the executive vice presidents and the CEO and make their case for why their numbers had come up short and why they hadn't met their objectives for the previous month. They pulled worried excuses out of their Resentments and Regrets sack one by one: sales couldn't serve customers because manufacturing made junk; manufacturing made junk because sales sold junk that manufacturing hadn't signed off on; engineering fussed about being kept out of the loop by both sales and manufacturing, so there was no way it could design better junk, and so on. Sound familiar yet?

Ironically, the more some of the participants emptied their sacks, the fuller those of others seemed to become. The executive vice presidents were increasingly irritated with the vice presidents and division heads, and the CEO got progressively more annoyed with everyone.

However, in an attempt to end on a good note and provide a glimmer of hope, each executive finished with a flourish, projecting unjustified numbers for the next month and a vague promise that better things would come. No one really believed the numbers or the promises, but at least it felt good to say it.

I know many of you have been to meetings of this type. They're not very productive, but they are somewhat entertaining in their own way, don't you think? (As long as your bonus isn't riding on the outcome.) It was no wonder that my client was stuck in neutral. The company spent 95 percent of its time rehashing and justifying the rubble of the past, and maybe 5 percent of its time identifying real rings of opportunity for the future.

And when the executives did focus on the future, they didn't fill their What If sacks with worries, they filled them with something maybe even more useless: costume jewelry, or fluffy, puffed-up numbers, and false promises that no one really believed. For the following month, everyone looked busy, but people weren't digging for opportunity so much as flinging dirt back and forth in preparation for next month's meeting—which, not surprisingly, was dreaded by everyone.

In this case, it wasn't change that was the issue; it was the *lack* of change that was causing the problem. The executives were so burdened by their sacks of Resentments and Regrets at what other departments had and hadn't done that they couldn't hope to discover and capitalize on new opportunities. It was the leader's job to break this downward spiral by insisting that people drop their sacks of Resentments and Regrets and get the group to collaborate—dig together—in a forward-moving, yet realistic direction toward new rings and new opportunities.

The same dynamic plays out in our personal lives. Once, as a psychology intern, I was providing marriage counseling to an older couple who had been married for quite some time. Our first session went something like this:

"How can I help you?" I asked. The wife answered first.

"Do you know what he did on our *honeymoon*?" she asked bitterly, leaning forward in her chair, eyes squinted, appearing eager to share her dismay. She then went on to describe a laundry list of offenses that he had committed during their first days and weeks together as a young married couple many years ago. She went on for some time.

The husband fussed and fidgeted through all this, and finally blurted out, "Well, I wouldn't have done any of that if you hadn't insisted that your mother come with us on the honeymoon!"

"How long have you two been married?" I asked out of curiosity.

"Thirty years," they responded.

I sat in stunned silence. It's an understatement to say that their sacks were full. Bitter resentments that had been stored up for 30 years came tumbling out. There was no stopping them. I tried to get them to focus on more recent events, but by the end of the first hour, I think we were up to week three of their obviously less than blissful 30 years of matrimony.

This couple was doing what many of us do: instead of letting their past go, they were using it as a weapon, continually beating each other over the head with their overburdened sacks of Resentments and Regrets, much as the executives had done to one another in our previous example. And when we do this, our professional and personal relationships suffer. And, when relationships suffer, teamwork and performance do too. At home, divorce rates go up, and at work, performance measures decline.

So how can we let go of the past? How can we lighten our load and grasp the ring by emptying our sacks of Resentments and Regrets and laying down our burdens? Or, better yet, how can we keep from filling our sacks in the first place? Admittedly, this can sometimes be a hard thing to do emotionally. However, the only thing that's harder and more damaging, both to ourselves and to our relationships at work and at home, is forever holding on to and weighing ourselves down with disappointments and pains from our past.

The first key to letting go is to fully experience whatever emotion it is that you are grappling with. Be aware of your emotions. Acknowledge them. Feel them. Major change often evokes strong emotions, and that's okay. Once the initial numbing shock of the change subsides, don't deny the emotions that follow. Anger, fear, sadness, and anxiety are common. Get it all out. Initially it may feel like these emotions are never-ending, but eventually you'll reach a calmer and more peaceful place within yourself if you don't fight what you are feeling.

There are many ways to bring these feelings to the forefront, as well as the thoughts that sustain them: talk to a trusted family member, friend, or coworker; get your thoughts and feelings out by putting them down on paper, maybe by keeping a journal or by writing a letter that's not meant to be sent, but simply expresses how you think and feel about a person or situation that's troubling you—write it, then destroy it; meditate or pray. Get out in nature if you can. Take a walk or a hike or a run. If you are at work, get out of the office on a break and take a stroll around the block. Make this a habit and you'll discard those troubles before they ever make it into your sack. As you're going through this process, be cognizant of others and be careful not to take your feelings out on them. If you are dealing with particularly weighty matters and feel that you need help in getting such things out in a healthy manner, seek professional counseling to work through them.

Eventually, by acknowledging and experiencing your negative thoughts and difficult feelings, you will let them go. The pain will subside, and you will again be able to latch on to the joys of the present. This is essential if you want to free up energy to snatch the ring out of the rubble. Again, begin to notice how your thoughts shape your feelings. Changing the way you think about a situation will help change the way you feel about it as well.

I'll always remember a beautiful young woman who approached me after one of my talks where I had shared these tools. She was crying and laughing all at once as she walked up to me. She said, "My husband died eight months ago. He was the light of my life, and then he was gone. But we had two children together. I've gradually come to realize that I can focus my love on them. And," she added, a big smile breaking through her tears, "the other thing I heard you say today was that it is all right to laugh again!"

With that we shared a hug and a hearty laugh together through both of our mounting tears. She demonstrated two keys to letting go: she experienced her emotions, and then she changed the way she looked at and thought about her situation. She told herself that it was okay to love and laugh again. In this way, she was digging through the rubble of her grief and finding new rings to enjoy once again.

Similar tools will help you empty your What If sack, which is filled with fears and worries about the future. The best way to empty your What If sack is to mentally stay in the present. Whenever you find yourself feeling nervous or anxious even though there is no immediate threat before you, your mind has probably fast-forwarded to something that hasn't happened yet. When this happens, bring yourself back to the present by asking yourself, "What's happening right here, right now?" You'll discover that often, whatever is going on right now isn't nearly as bad as the future you're imagining.

For example, let's say you lose your job today. Panic sets in. *What if I can't pay my bills? What if I lose my house? What if my spouse leaves me (or comes back!)?* Stop and think. You're not likely to end up homeless tomorrow. You still have a roof over your head and the ability to look for a new job. If funds are tight, by all means go on a budget, but recognize that all is not lost in this moment. Rather than waste energy worrying about not having a job, pour that energy into finding another one.

Certainly, these worries are normal, and you can expect negative emotions to creep in regardless. That's part of the rubble. Change brings uncertainty, and often uncertainty brings fear. The key is to not let that fear immobilize you, but use it as energy to propel you forward. Mentally stay in the moment and the What If sack won't become too full.

To keep yourself free from the burdens that hold you down and hold you back, practice letting go of both resentments from the past and worries about the future. It's important to learn from the past, but not live in it; to plan for the future, but not act as if the worst-case scenario has already played out. In this way, you will empty your sacks and keep them from filling back up. Letting go frees you to grab the rings of opportunity that change always creates, whether it's a chance for a better situation at work or opportunities for better relationships and more happiness at home.

DIG A LITTLE
DEEPER

1. *What are you holding on to that in reality is holding you down or holding you back?*

2. *What are you worrying about incessantly that hasn't happened yet?*

3. *What do you gain by holding on to the past or worrying about the future?*

4. *Are you willing to feel vulnerable by setting down your sacks? Ultimately, who is hurt if you refuse to surrender them?*

5. *What is one thing that you can do in the next 24 hours that will lighten your load? Write it down and/or tell someone about it to help hold yourself accountable for carrying it out.*

Chapter Three

LATCH ON TO WHAT MATTERS MOST

I decided to be with my son during this critical time, focusing my thoughts on the present and on what I could affect at that very moment, rather than fretting about the circumstances of his birth or worrying about what might happen next. My love for him became paramount. This simple act and clear frame of mind gave me the courage I needed to see this crisis through.

Do you have an old shoebox stashed away some-place, maybe under the bed or in your bedroom closet? Maybe it's in your basement or garage. Whatever the container and wherever you keep it, this is the place where you store your personal and particu-lar—and sometimes peculiar—treasures or personal heirlooms. These items are rarely valuable to anyone other than you, and their monetary value may be minimal, but you treasure them nevertheless. Personal heirlooms are valuable because they are reminders of what matters most in life. During difficult changes, they conjure up feelings of happier, more secure times.

And, perhaps most importantly, when the waves of change crash about us, heirlooms represent a steady platform above the fray, a place deep in our soul that never changes, to which we can always retreat to find some measure of safety, comfort, and guidance. Because of this, we carefully preserve these heirlooms and take them with us wherever we go. The feelings they engender are eternal, and no one can wrest them away. They are external symbols of the internal values that matter most to us.

In business, we have heirlooms, too. You'll find them in different forms and places, but almost every business has them. Maybe it's the first dollar earned that's hanging on the pizzeria's or ice cream parlor's wall; maybe it's the corridor at corporate headquarters where pictures and artifacts from the past are displayed with pride; maybe it's a frayed newspaper or magazine article about the organization's founding or its philanthropic ventures that is carefully preserved and displayed in a place of prominence.

Like personal heirlooms, these business heirlooms rarely have large monetary value, but they are incredibly valuable nevertheless, because they come to represent the organization's underlying values; they reinforce and help institutionalize the company's culture. The values may center on taking risks, taking care of the customer, or concern for the environment. They might represent the ability to create consistent shareholder return or to be a good corporate neighbor involved in the community. These values are heirlooms in that they represent what matters most to a particular organization and the people who work there.

It is important that a company's heirlooms be preserved because often they become embedded in the business's brand and are seared into the collective unconscious of its customers. Destroy them at your peril.

In many ways, these images and associated feelings *are* the brand, and they are extremely valuable. For example, when Coca-Cola introduced its "new Coke" product, the company discovered that for many people, the original Coca-Cola was also a treasured family heirloom. Today, the company's leaders are working hard to preserve this perception.

Indeed, safeguarding the values personified by a company's brand or image is the responsibility of each succeeding generation of leaders in all organizations. That's because in a world of nearly constant change, *effective leaders recognize that values are the one thing in an organization that should never change, and that it is their responsibility to preserve and protect them.*

In his bestselling book *Good to Great*, Jim Collins established that one of the factors that distinguish companies that lasted for generations from those that gradually disappeared is that the former were founded on a set of corporate values that have remained constant since the company's inception. Products change, markets change, and people change, but in companies with impressive records of sustainability and longevity, values don't change.

In other words, *a company without enduring values will not be able to produce long-term value.* I'm not referring to those values stated on a plaque on the wall following a one-time executive retreat. Such statements often reflect flavor-of-the-month thinking at best, and shallow insincerity at worst.

True values are long-lasting and live beyond the people who first conceived of them and gave them a voice. I once heard a poignant tale about this specific point. Early in his career, a senior executive recognized that values were an important aspect of successful businesses. So, when he got promoted and took over a division, he articulated the new values that he brought with him to everyone in the division. He trumpeted these values wherever he went, and he even had them etched into the glass over the doorways on every floor.

A year or two later, the executive in question got transferred. Before he left, he was walking down the hall one day and saw workmen on ladders working with razor blades on the glass over the doors. As he got closer, to his horror and dismay, he saw that they were literally erasing the values he had worked so hard to inculcate. This painful example underscores the fact that true corporate values represent much more than the good ideas of any one person at a particular time.

Values are collective and enduring beliefs about what matters most in how to conduct business from day to day, from year to year, and beyond. They permeate every aspect of an organization and outlive the people who work there. These corporate heirlooms become the organization's glue, connecting past generations with succeeding ones. More importantly, these un-changing, enduring values become a source of practical guidance in times of difficult change when the company's leaders are forced to make difficult decisions without a safety net.

The classic example of this is the Tylenol tampering scare in 1982 that led to several deaths in the Chicago area. Executives at Johnson & Johnson, the maker of Tylenol, reacted quickly by standing on the unwavering platform of values established by the company's founders years before the crisis. They recalled the prod-uct, cooperated with investigators, and gave the media full disclosure. By taking responsibility, they eventually turned the rubble of a potentially crippling PR crisis into a ring of better product safety and a positive public image for the company.

How many times have we seen just the opposite? A company gets caught in a difficult situation, and rather than rush to resolve it, the executives run for cover. Rather than stand up and take responsibility, they hun-ker down and start pointing fingers. There's no need to cite any one particular company; we've all seen this happen too many times.

The same applies to individuals at work, too. The best leaders always stand by their values. They let their standards dictate their actions rather than following the whims of popular passions. In contrast, poor leaders choose the popular response that might be expedient, but is wrong.

So, one of the best ways to handle constant change is to be clear about your unwavering values. The first step is to establish these principles; you can't adhere to a set of values if you don't know what they are. During times of change, these ethics become beacons as you consider the actions and next steps that need to be taken.

Here's a simple exercise to help you identify your own set of values. Imagine that from this moment forward, you were never able to go back to your current place of employment again, not even to say good-bye. Now, after some of you get through jumping for joy, ask yourself what you would specifically miss about the place where you work right now other than a paycheck. Take some time to really think this through. What would you miss the most?

Would it be the people and the relationships you have built with them over time? Would it be the sense of accomplishment and achievement that comes when you set and reach your goals? Would it be contributing to a winning team? Would it be the challenge of succeeding in a constantly changing environment? Or would it be something else? I propose that whatever you would miss most represents what you value most—it represents your work-related heirloom. Having established these guideposts, you'll be ready when change comes along, as it inevitably will, and you will find solace in your internal values. Even if you lose your job or switch companies or careers, these values or heirlooms will go with you, providing emotional comfort and practical guidance when you need them most.

I recently attended a sales meeting where management announced that major changes to the compensation and rewards package were underway but were not yet complete. Tension began to fill the room as members of the sales force began to worry that the changes might have a negative impact on their annual compensation. A somewhat contentious question and answer session seemed to only fuel their anxiety, since the presiding executives did not have all the answers to their detailed questions. Finally, one of the executives stepped to the microphone and said:

"It's true that we are changing your compensation package and that all of the details won't be worked out for another few months. But it's also true that we are not changing, nor will we ever change, our long-held stance of valuing employees and treating them fairly. I can assure you that, driven by these values, we will not design a system that will ultimately do you harm. That simply is not our way. And you can hold me to that." With that, the reduction of tension in the room was palpable. I could sense that people trusted this executive and that he meant what he said. Falling back on fundamental, unchanging values helped him navigate a steady course to help his people through an unsettling and uncertain time of change.

In the same way, you should rely on your values when you initiate personal change, such as considering different career paths or new job opportunities. Your values act as a compass to guide you toward the professional opportunities that foster and reinforce what it is about work and life that you value the most. I remember meeting a first-shift factory worker who had a degree from MIT. Curious, I asked him why he had not pursued a management track or some other position that might place more value on his education. To him, it was all about values.

He said, "Sometimes I think about that when I'm driving my 10-year-old jalopy, and I get to thinking of my brother the doctor driving his Mercedes. But I decided a long time ago that spending time with my family is what is most important to me. My brother might drive a nicer car, like some of the guys in management do here. But I look at the hours they have to work and what they have to put up with to do it. My job is low stress, and I get off every day at 3:30. I get to go home and be with my family. I have three kids, and I coach each of their sports teams and get to spend time with my wife. You don't get a second chance to be a parent to your kids when they're growing up. So yeah, sometimes I wonder if maybe I should do something else, but it always comes back to family, and that's what matters most to me. So I'm happy doing what I'm doing. Maybe when they're grown I'll consider doing something else."

It's simple: do what you value, and you will value what you do. It may seem strange in a book about change to spend an entire chapter on things that should never be altered, but it is those very valuable heirlooms that we can turn to for solace, guidance, and comfort when we need them most—when forces of change that are beyond our control have reduced our best-laid plans to rubble once again.

DIG A LITTLE DEEPER

1. *Why do you get up and go to work each day other than to receive a paycheck?*

2. *If you could never return to where you work right now, what would you miss most?*

3. *What are the fundamental values that have driven your company/division/department in the past and will always drive it in the future?*

4. *What would your values have you do in a specific change situation that you face right now?*

5. *Do you believe that you need to hire people with the right values already, or that you can train people to have the necessary values to be successful in your particular company and culture? Discuss or debate this question with a colleague, or as a team.*

Chapter Four

DON'T MANAGE TIME, INVEST IT IN PEOPLE

In my professional life, I was unable to go to the office, and I didn't know how long this would continue. We were a small firm, and I had commitments to honor. Thankfully, my boss never said a word about my missing work. He gave me the space to do what I needed to do for my family, yet I knew he trusted me to meet my responsibilities to my clients. Personally, people all around the country were praying for my family. My wife and I were bolstered by the collective efforts of the countless friends, family, and colleagues who kept us in their thoughts and prayers.

C hange management on a broad scale is a logical process. It's all about planning, structure, systems, broad communication and detailed organization. Change *leadership* on any scale is a psychological process. It's all about the trust, caring, and honest communication that underlie all successful human relationships. Very few people will follow you into the rubble, or give you their best effort once they're there, if you haven't established a trusting relationship with them first.

The message of this chapter is simple: to better lead change in the future, build better relationships with your upcoming *ringleaders* now. When change hits, ringleaders are the folks you can count on to pick up a shovel without being told. And, they are the ones that others willingly follow into the pile time and again to search for the ring. Identifying and building strong working relationships with your company's ringleaders is crucial. Don't wait until change is upon you to establish these relationships—by then it is too late. It's imperative that you invest time in these people now if you want them to support you later by leading others to search for the ring.

In business, the soft skills are the ones that are hard to master. They're difficult for some who find building relationships uncomfortable, and they're time-intensive. Yet it is the soft skills that build a strong business foundation and corporate culture—and they are a company's last competitive advantage. Without solid working relationships based on trust and mutual respect, hard results are difficult to produce on a consistent basis.

Let me ask you, have you ever gotten so mad at work that you felt like beating someone up? Many of you might say, "Well, sure, several times a day!" Here's a story of someone who actually did it, and his story illustrates my point about the importance of relationship building and leading change.

Steve Smith is an outstanding professional football player for the National Football League's Carolina Panthers. Once, early in his career, Steve became so angry in a team meeting that he physically attacked a teammate and beat him so severely that the teammate had to go to the hospital for treatment. The team's response was to suspend Steve for just one game.

My son and I were fans of the team, and when I heard about this punishment, I felt it was exceedingly light and represented poor values on the part of team management. I resented having to explain those values to my son. So I Googled the name of the team owner, discovered that it was a man named Jerry Richardson, and proceeded to write him an angry letter about the situation. I didn't hear anything back from Mr. Richardson, nor did I expect to. I guessed that my letter was sitting on a customer service rep's desk on its way into the trash. Several months passed, and the football season ended.

I came home from the gym one day and my wife said, "Look what came in while you were out." And there was a faxed copy of my letter to Jerry Richardson, owner of the Carolina Panthers. On it was this handwritten note: "I have received your letter. Steve Smith and I would like to come and visit with you and your son. I will call at 10 a.m. to discuss." The note was signed, "Jerry Richardson."

"Right," I said. "Like Jerry Richardson actually wrote this note. Which one of my buddies got hold of this letter?" I was sure it was a hoax and waited for the call. The phone rang right at ten.

"Hello, Gary? This is Jerry Richardson," a gruff voice said.

"Right, and this is the Easter Bunny," I answered. "Who is this really? Bob, is that you?"

"It's Jerry Richardson," the gruff voice said again. "Steve Smith and I would like to come visit with you and your son."

It didn't sound like Bob or any other of my buddies, and I began to entertain the notion that maybe it really was Jerry Richardson. But why would he be calling me?

"So what's the purpose of your call?" I asked.

"I already told you. Steve Smith and I want to come and visit you and your son!"

Now it was his turn to get agitated. My mind was racing. This made no sense. Nevertheless, Mr. Richardson and I set a date for him and Steve to come visit with my son and me. I hung up the phone and turned to my wife.

"This doesn't make any sense. Why would an NFL owner and one of his best players come all this way (we lived 100 miles from team headquarters) just to visit with one fan and his son? They're not going to do that."

"Maybe it's a publicity stunt," Peggy offered. "He'll probably arrive with a reporter and photographer, and they'll try to write a feel-good story and get a little positive PR for the team."

That made sense, but I was still dubious. I called up my older brother Jeff to see what he thought. (*Note:* Never call your brother in these types of situations.) "Oh, I know why they are coming, all right," Jeff said with conviction immediately after I explained the situation to him.

"You do? Tell me!" I demanded anxiously.

"It's obvious. They're coming to beat the crap out of you too!" he said.

"Thanks a lot, big brother," I said, hanging up the phone.

Still, I had to admit that that idea made more sense than anything else I had come up with. The day for the visit arrived, and it was snowing. *Well, there's their out,* I thought. *They'll never come now.* But come they did. They drove through the snow, and they ended up spending three hours with us. Steve took my son to lunch at McDonald's, then they went back to my house, where Steve let my son whip him in foosball. Mr. Richardson and I went to a local restaurant, where he explained the purpose of his visit.

He started off by apologizing for not getting back to me sooner, but explained that, unbeknownst to me, he had been in the hospital when my letter came and he had spent the next several months recuperating. He was just now getting around to catching up with his backlog of business. He went on to say that he wanted to explain to me why the team took the action that it did with Steve and what the plan was for monitoring the situation going forward.

He said also that he wanted me to have a chance to meet Steve for myself, adding that he didn't make Steve come, that Steve had decided to make the visit on his own. I admired Steve greatly for that, and I still do. Turns out that he's a good man who made a bad mistake and has tried to learn about the aspects of his character that led him to do it. We can all learn something from that.

Needless to say, I was astounded. I still couldn't believe that an NFL owner and one of his best players, who must have had better things to do with their time, would spend their whole day visiting with one fan and his son. When I asked about this, Mr. Richardson responded, "Well, you were angry, and we don't like unhappy customers."

"But I must not have been the only one. I am sure you got other angry letters about Steve's situation."

"We did."

"So why me? Why did you choose to come visit me?"

Leaning in, he looked me right in the eye, with a gleam in his. "You were *really* angry!"

This story speaks volumes about caring about your customers, having a passion for doing things right and doing the right things, and investing time in people. It wasn't until almost a year later that I realized how powerful this story was as it relates to change leadership and lessons for proactively cultivating change.

The Panthers went on to the Super Bowl the following season, and Steve Smith emerged as a team leader—a ringleader. At the end of the season, the press quoted him as saying that he wanted to stay with the Carolina Panthers even though his contract was up. I was surprised, because most players don't like to declare their intentions publicly before negotiating a deal with the team.

Suddenly my mind flashed back to the day, now almost a year earlier, when Steve and Mr. Richardson had visited with my son and me. Immediately, I saw that visit in a totally different light. Mr. Richardson hadn't just invested his time in a fan and his son that day. He had done that, to be sure, but he had done much more than that. He had invested his time in one of his key players, one that he knew could become a ringleader on a team that was poised to seize the golden ring of a Super Bowl run and potential championship.

All it took was a little investment in time between the two in order to sow the seeds of a stronger working relationship later; one based on mutual trust and respect. Mr. Richardson and Steve spent several hours in the car that day driving back and forth. I can only imagine the things they talked about and how that helped cement their working relationship. Out of that relationship came a run at the Super Bowl and several solid seasons thereafter.

The moral of the story is to figure out who your Steve Smiths are; these are your diamonds in the rough—people with the potential to emerge as future ringleaders if you can give them time and attention now. Identify them and invest in them; they will help lead your organization toward whatever the Super Bowl is for your industry.

There are many ways to discover the diamonds in the rough working in your organization. The simplest approach is to get out and meet them. Use the old Tom Peters technique of Management by Walking Around, with the intent of finding these uncut jewels. Get out of your comfort zone. Resist the temptation to visit only with folks you already know or to build relationships only with those at your organizational level. Move up and down the organizational ladder. For example, if you work in the office, visit the warehouse. You never know whom you might meet or what you will discover about your company, its culture, and its people.

I was speaking with a business owner recently who told me that he had been regularly criticized by employees who were upset with the returns they were getting on the 401(k) he was managing for them. Then the owner learned of one employee who was working in the warehouse. This man had retired from a successful career and had taken the warehouse job just to keep busy. With a little digging, the owner discovered that in the man's previous career, he was a successful money manager for a major brokerage firm. A diamond in the rough— and a ring to boot! "Now they're beating him up!" the owner said with a smile.

Here's another technique for discovering your uncut diamonds: in a series of management meetings, set aside some time for each member of the team to identify and discuss the merits and demerits of the best and worst leaders he or she has found in their *colleagues'* divisions and departments. This technique helps avoid the blind spots we all tend to have for our own organization, favorite colleague, or protégé.

With both techniques, make sure you dig down several layers into the organization. Remember that leadership is not defined by position or rank, it's defined by whether or not you have followers—those who trust you and are loyal to you, and who will join you in the hunt for the ring, no matter how difficult the circumstances. To paraphrase Franklin Delano Roosevelt, it's a bad feeling as a leader to look over your shoulder and see that no one is following.

So find out which people are being followed and why, no matter what these people's level. Once you've identified them, it's time for polishing and refinement. Make sure that all of these diamonds in the rough are getting the attention they deserve, both from you and from others who are in a position to facilitate their career growth and development. Encourage these people to dig in search of opportunities for themselves and the organization. Send them to courses and industry conferences. Give them exposure and expand their influence by having them lead high-visibility project teams that will drive the business forward. Find ways to spend time with them informally. Take them to lunch or for a bite after work.

Will such efforts always pay off? No. There are no guarantees; all investments carry a certain amount of risk. You may find that you invested time in certain people, and it didn't work out; perhaps the diamond had serious flaws that were previously undetected. That's to be expected. It always makes sense to develop several ringleaders and not put the hopes of your organization on the shoulders of just one individual. It's similar to creating a diversified financial portfolio; distributing your investments over a variety of investment vehicles helps ensure that your overall returns will hold up under the pressure of surprising market shifts and unanticipated change.

So never stop searching for that next uncut diamond, and never stop investing in those that you uncover. As

Jerry Richardson and Steve Smith demonstrated, a little investment now can pay great dividends later on. Keep in mind that there will never be a good time to make all of this happen. Pressing matters spring up every day that will drain your time, energy, and attention from your intention to invest in people. Like financial investing, investing in people takes discipline. Add it as a specific "to-do" in your calendar.

And finally, don't delegate this important task. Don't try to slough it off on someone else or on another department like Human Resources. HR certainly has an important part to play in this endeavor, but you need to take control.

Jerry Richardson responded directly to Steve and me. He didn't send an emissary. We both got the message, because he did.

DIG A LITTLE DEEPER

1. *Have you made an effort to get to know people outside the circle that you interact with every day? If not, why not? What steps can you take to uncover these diamonds in the rough and begin building these relationships?*

2. *What's the "Super Bowl" in your industry, and who are the "Steve Smiths" or future ringleaders that you can count on to lead you to that ring? Write down their names.*

3. *How can you better invest in these players now? How can you challenge and stimulate them to grow?*

4. *Do you delegate investing time in people to others in your organization? How can you personally give more of yourself in the form of time and attention to cement the bonds of loyalty between you and the key players in your organization?*

5. *Are you willing to invest time and money in the "soft stuff" to get better results with the "hard stuff"? What are the risks if you don't make these investments?*

Chapter Five

Don't Forget to Invest in Your Precious Gems at Home

The statistics were frightening. I read somewhere that an estimated 90 percent of marriages end in divorce when there is a chronically ill child involved. I could believe it. Peggy and I were emotionally torn and tattered. Physically, too. The days were long, and the news was constantly bad. It was a fragile and uncertain time. I couldn't predict which way it would turn out, and for a guy like me who always likes to control things, that was really tough. The rubble was deep, and there seemed to be no ring in sight.

As I mentioned earlier, a critical part of creating a healthy financial portfolio is diversifying your investments. A healthy mix of stocks, bonds, and mutual funds helps mitigate the effects of changing and unpredictable markets. It works the same way with your Change Portfolio, a metaphor I use to describe the investment of time and energy you make in people.

A healthy Change Portfolio includes diversified investments in not only your diamonds in the rough at work, but your precious gems at home. These are the individuals—friends and family—that you hold most dear outside of work. They are the ones you count on to pick you up when change gets you down. It's easy to take these folks for granted and to neglect your investment in them. For that matter, it's easy to take *ourselves* for granted and neglect those investments, too.

How many of us put our needs, and those of our families, behind those of our business, customers, and clients? We trust that our family and friends will always be there for us, but we aren't so sure about our clients and customers, so sometimes we put them first. And, we reason that if we don't take care of business first, we won't be able to take care of our family, at least financially. So for many of us, work is the priority. There is some merit to this line of reasoning, but there is danger in it because it leads to an unbalanced portfolio. An unbalanced portfolio is much more vulnerable to the vagaries of unanticipated change.

I discovered this principle in a most unusual and poignant manner. When I was in graduate school, I was assigned as the psychology intern on the physical rehabilitation floor of a large medical hospital. I vividly remember an elderly, powerful, and proud gentleman who was admitted because he had suffered a stroke that had left him permanently paralyzed in one arm. My job was to address his emotional needs during his stay.

I visited his room every day for two weeks, but I got nowhere. He wouldn't speak a word to me. Finally, one day, as I was searching for a topic to engage him, I asked, "Sir, you have been here for two weeks, but I don't recall you having any visitors during that time. Don't you have any family nearby?" The old and prideful man stared straight ahead with a steely gaze, saying nothing. Then I noticed a large tear forming in the corner of one eye and slowly rolling down his face.

Still, he said nothing. I waited.

Finally, the old man turned toward me. His voice was deep, and quiet. He spoke slowly.

"Son, I never needed nobody. I lived for myself and by myself. I figured everybody else could do the same. I especially didn't want any family members come snooping around looking for money. I worked, unlike some of them. So, I had nothing to do with 'em. And they had nothing to do with me. That's the way I liked it. That's the way I wanted it. You asked if I have family around here? I have *12* family members who live within *three* blocks of this hospital. But none of them have come to visit me, and none of them will. And I don't blame them. I never treated 'em right, and now they'll never want anything to do with me again."

He finished. We were both quiet for a while. Then I asked, "You mentioned you had a job before the stroke and the paralysis. Will you be able to go back to that at least?"

"I moved pianos," he said.

This patient had neglected his Change Portfolio, and little could help him now. If you don't make your investments in those who are close to you in your personal life, the safety net that you rely on during difficult periods will cease to exist. You'll be left to deal with change and its consequences on your own. That's a lonely and sad situation, and all too common. Some of us pay a hefty price for our success at work when we neglect to invest in our precious gems at home.

Sometimes it's not a lack of investment in our precious gems that creates trouble, but rather trying to do too much. It's like being a day trader who's out of control. We get so busy trying to create opportunities that we end up creating rubble instead. We lose sight of the ring we were searching for in the first place. And instead of finding it, we pile more and more rubble on top.

How many of you want to give your kids (or your grandkids, nieces, or nephews) every opportunity to grow up and be successful in whatever life they choose? You want to give them more than what you had growing up, even if what you had growing up was satisfactory. Either way, you want to give them every possible ring of opportunity that's within your power. So you sign them up for music lessons, private schools, tutoring, and athletic programs. Often, they end up in activities that require meetings or practice several nights a week, and overnight travel on the weekends. The financial and emotional price is high. Between the kids' schedule and yours, family life becomes a whirlwind of out-of-control activity.

Your marriage is transformed into a tag team chauffeuring service. Communication between you and your spouse consists mostly of an exchange of information about who's going where and who's doing what over the next several days and weeks. As for investing in yourself by going to the gym or reading a book or eating a healthier diet, forget about it. You decide that all those gurus who write the self-help books and articles about work-life balance don't have either kids or jobs, or both.

To find the ring in this rubble, you have to rebalance your Change Portfolio. As with financial investments, periodically you need to reexamine your goals in life and make sure that your current investments of time and energy are in line with those goals.

Sometimes getting a reminder helps. As a young leadership consultant, I was always on the go, building my business to support my family. One night, after a quick dinner with the family sandwiched between business meetings, I got up to leave.

"Where are you going?" my six-year-old asked, his face flashing concern.

"Daddy has a business meeting."

"But you just got home!"

"I'll only be gone a few hours. I promise I'll give you a good night kiss when I get back."

"But I'll be asleep," he protested, his concern mounting.

Suddenly he cried, "Wait a minute!" and raced out of the room. Soon he came running back and handed me his picture.

"Here," he sniffed, the tears welling up. "Take this picture to remember me by!"

Okay, so the kid had a flair for the dramatic, but I got the message. I had been working a lot back then, and I had not been home much the previous several weeks. My son missed me and needed me, and as I thought about it at the time, I missed him and needed him too. Not to mention the time I was missing with my wife and daughter too. I had been neglecting my investments at home. Without being aware of it, I had allowed work to consume me. My son's theatrics woke me up to the need for rebalancing my Change Portfolio to align it with my life goal of putting family before business whenever possible.

Now, I know some of you are thinking that because you work for somebody else, you don't have the luxury of putting off business obligations or taking time off frequently, that your company won't allow it. Sometimes that's true. Some organizations are miserly with giving us time off, but remember: even Bob Cratchitt asked for and got time off at Christmas! Don't let your fears about what your company will or won't allow become an excuse for not administering your Change Portfolio.

I always remember what one executive in a professional services firm taught me about this. Her firm was notorious for people complaining about their lack of life balance and blaming their condition on their employer and highly demanding clients. When I asked this executive about it, she said, "If I'm at a client site and I believe I need to get home for an important family event, no one from my firm or the client is going to stop me. At the same time, I don't expect them to drive me to the airport!"

The personal responsibility she took is right on target. We are all responsible for where we choose to invest our time and energy. That doesn't mean that we always get to do what we want and can avoid making any sacrifices. It simply means that when and where to make such sacrifices is ultimately an individual choice.

And, just like our investments in people at work, it's easy to put off our investments in those at home. You get busy and believe that you'll get to it later, but if you hesitate, you might not get another chance. A bittersweet example: recently, I endured the toughest day of my professional career, a day that was at once one of the saddest and one of the most rewarding experiences I've had in quite a while.

I was preparing to give a speech scheduled for the following day when the phone rang in my hotel room. It was my client. "Gary, can you come down to the lobby and meet with us? We've had a horrible tragedy." When I went downstairs, my client informed me that one of their top executives had died that morning during the meeting. The executive, I'll call her Linda Ann, was scheduled to be the next speaker. She was all miked up and ready to go, but she never made it to the podium. Within moments, she collapsed and was gone.

Rather than give my speech the next morning, I helped preside over an impromptu memorial service instead. Linda Ann was 41 years old, had been married five years, had no children, and had been in seemingly good health. So where in the world was the ring in that rubble?

First, the rubble was very deep and very painful. It was a tragic and devastating turn of events. The pain was intense, powerful, and palpable—even for me, a virtual outsider. I could only imagine what it was like for those who knew her, worked with her, and loved her. But as I spent time with this group over the next 24 hours, it became clear that the ring came from Linda Ann herself, in the form of the legacy she left behind.

Everyone I spoke with said that they knew, liked, and admired Linda Ann. She always had a smile on her face, right up until the moment she died. One executive said that Linda Ann was the kind of person who could tell you no and make you feel good about it. "I could be having the worst day of my life, and after talking to Linda Ann, I would walk away feeling how lucky I was to be having that day," he said.

Another told me of a grueling feedback exercise he had gone through as part of his career development. He had had to meet with several senior executives. Apparently they had showed him no mercy. "By the time I got to Linda Ann, I was pretty beat up," he said. "I sat down and braced myself for another round of punishment. Instead, Linda Ann took one look at me and said, 'You don't look like you need any more feedback. How about a cookie instead?' We sat back and broke bread together. She was the best."

In sharing their pain, Linda Ann's coworkers remembered the joy she had brought to each one, and the executive skill and talent she had contributed to the company. It was clear that she was both loved as a person and respected as a professional by her colleagues and coworkers. Yes, Linda Ann was gone, but thanks to the investments she had made in people, her legacy of contagious energy, achieving results, and enjoying every step along the way lived on. Her legacy *was* the ring in the rubble.

And that brings us full circle in the soft stuff–versus–hard stuff debate. My point is this: investing in relationships is a soft activity, but it is a necessary one if you want to deliver consistently good, hard, visible results at work. And, if you achieve good results at work but pay little attention to your investments at home, what have you really gained in the end? Who is going to be there to share the joy with you when things go well? And who will rescue you from the rubble when they don't? As I see it, it's not an either/or proposition; it's clear to me that you can't do either one consistently well without doing both.

DIG A LITTLE DEEPER

1. Make a list of your precious gems at home. Are you investing the time in them that you and they might want?

2. How balanced is your Change Portfolio? Do you have a healthy mix of investments inside and outside of work, including investments in your physical, mental, spiritual, and social well-being?

3. What can you do to get your Portfolio more in balance? What are your typical excuses, and what trade-offs will you make to overcome them?

4. What legacy would you leave if for whatever reason you left work or your family tomorrow? What would people say about you? How comfortable are you with that? What can you do right now to alter that course?

5. Think of someone you know who seems to have a Change Portfolio that's in balance. What can you emulate about them?

Chapter Six

REPEAT AFTER ME: YOU ARE NOT THE CENTER OF THE UNIVERSE

The medical team was working feverishly to save my son's life. Periodically someone came out to give me updates. Once, a doctor on the team emerged, beaming a smile. "Good news!" he exclaimed. "Your son has a brain!" "What!?" "Your son has a brain," he repeated. "With all due respect," I asked, "what are you talking about?" He went on to explain that children who were born this ill were sometimes found to have no brain, just a brain stem. "But," he added proudly, almost smugly, "we just did a CT scan, and your son has a complete brain." I was dumbfounded. "Great," I finally managed to sputter. "He's one step ahead of his old man." With a chuckle, I added, "Would you please go back in there and find out what's wrong with my son?" It was good to find that I hadn't lost my sense of humor.

Why is it that when you give a small child a gift, he often drives you nuts by wanting to play with the box rather than the very expensive toy it contained (a toy that you probably waited forever in line to buy)? It's because the child doesn't see the box as merely a container and then trash, like you do; he sees it as an extension of the gift itself. He does not yet share your belief, so it hasn't shaped his worldview. Therefore, the box can become anything to the child. To him, it can be a chair, a helmet, a house, or a handy projectile. The message in this chapter is that without preconceived beliefs about the way things are, there are no limits to what you can accomplish and to the positive changes you can impart.

As adults, most of us go through life carefully focused on our own little worlds. We tend to think that what we see is reality, and to forget that there is a much bigger world out there that, if we considered it, would put our situation into perspective. When we forget this, we tend to take our own perspective a little too seriously, and in the process, we take ourselves too seriously as well. In effect, we become the center of our own universe.

What results is an inability to deal with change; when it comes along and disrupts our worldview, we may come to think, feel, and act as if the world has come to an end. We lose perspective, and with this mindset, the negative effects of change become exaggerated in our minds and in our experience, sometimes leaving us feeling overwhelmed and unable to cope as effectively as we might have done otherwise. Similarly, we feel unable to make change happen. We get the false sense that we have to accept that "that's the way things are," and we become blind to our own ability to effect positive change.

One of the best ways to counter this trend is to discover, nourish, and enjoy our sense of humor. Humor with a touch of self-deprecation is the antidote to taking yourself too seriously. And taken together, humor and humility provide protection against the stress and pressure of change. Armed with a sense of humor and a healthy perspective, you are in a much better position to lead yourself and others through difficult change. Which would you rather follow: someone who radiates a sense of confidence and composure, or someone who always fears the worst and is quick to cry, "The sky is falling!"?

In fact, a review of American history reveals that many of the presidents who led the nation through dramatic and sweeping change had a well-honed sense of humor. Abraham Lincoln, Franklin Delano Roosevelt, John F. Kennedy, and Ronald Reagan were all known for putting others at ease through well-timed and good-natured jokes, quips, and stories. In this way, they released the pressure and tension of constant and often unpredictable change, for themselves and their followers. The strategy of blending humor with humility makes good business sense, too. A company culture that fosters these characteristics creates a carryover effect for its customers that's just good business.

A prime example comes from an organization I recently ran across called CD Baby. I had gone to the company's Web site to purchase a couple of CDs. Below is a transcript of the e-mail I received from the company confirming that my order had been shipped. I read it with growing surprise and delight:

Your CDs have been gently taken from our CD Baby shelves with sterilized contamination-free gloves and placed on a satin pillow.

A team of 50 employees inspected your CDs and polished them to make sure they were in the best possible condition before mailing.

Our packaging specialist from Japan lit a candle and a hush fell over the crowd as he put your CDs into the finest gold-lined box that money can buy.

We all had a wonderful celebration afterwards and the whole party marched down the street to the post office where the entire town of Portland waved "Bon Voyage!" to your package, on its way to you, in our private CD Baby jet.

I hope you had a wonderful time shopping at CD Baby. We sure did. Your picture is on our wall as "Customer of the Year." We're all exhausted but can't wait for you to come back to CDBABY. COM!!

I have no doubt that the staff members of CD Baby would be able to roll with almost any situation, regardless of the changes that might come their way. Not taking themselves too seriously keeps the company nimble enough to quickly adjust to new and unexpected circumstances, rather than laboring under the weight of a more serious and ponderous business culture. To see what I mean, go to the company's Web site. The staff members clearly don't take themselves too seriously, and they'll lighten your burdens by providing a relaxed place to do business. Visit the company's Web site and you'll immediately feel the stress of your day begin to melt under the onslaught of the staff members' relentless good humor. Stress relief through good humor is an added benefit of doing business with CD Baby. And who knows, you just might buy a CD while you're there.

In summary, if you escape from the limitations imposed by your own static and insular thinking, you are better equipped to find the ring in any change. And you don't need to be a professional comedian to adopt this attitude and infuse it within your organization. You do need to take a step or two outside of your comfort zone and develop a realistic and less serious sense of yourself.

Take Randall, for example. I met him in a leadership program I had conducted some time ago. Randall was one of the most serious and buttoned-up CEOs you'd ever want to meet. And I mean literally buttoned-up: every day he wore a coat and tie to the program, which was more of a khakis and polo shirt type of event. Frankly, I wasn't sure how much Randall had benefited from the program. His stony expression and taciturn demeanor didn't change much over the course of the weeklong program. He emoted very little and said even less. Even as a trained psychologist, I found him to be a tough man to read. It wasn't until one of his vice presidents attended the program a few months later that I realized that Randall had taken some of the things we had covered to heart after all.

"What did you guys do to Randall?" the vice president asked me as soon as he arrived at the program. "Did you brainwash him or something?"

"Uh-oh, why?"

"No, I mean he came back different, but in a good kind of way."

"Tell me."

"When Randall got back, we had our monthly management meeting. Only, this time Randall had stripped the boardroom of all the furniture: tables, chairs, even the clock on the wall—everything. When we walked in for the three-hour meeting, there was nothing but Randall, us, the floor, and the four walls."

"What did you do?"

"We didn't know what to do; we were shocked. Then Randall sat down on the floor in full coat and tie. Normally, he is about as serious and formal as it gets. And now he's sitting on the floor in the middle of this empty boardroom? We couldn't believe what we were seeing."

"What happened?"

"Well, before you know it, we were all on the floor, loosening our ties and getting comfortable as best we could. It turned out to be one of the best meetings we have had in a long, long time. People were more open, and the conversation seemed to flow more freely than usual. We got issues on the table and dealt with stuff we'd normally avoid. I think that by sitting on the floor, people were less intimidated by Randall than they usually are. Plus, we didn't have a table to hide behind. It put all of us on a more even plane. We were more relaxed, and that really seemed to get us going."

Randall is a perfect example of someone who has developed a strong understanding of himself and recognizes the importance of not taking oneself too seriously in reaching out to a broad spectrum of people. Once you expand your periphery and develop loyal followers by becoming more approachable through humor and humility, your entire team will be better able to devise new and creative ways to dig for the ring. Adding a measure of humor and humility to your everyday outlook will help you keep the rubble in your life in its proper place while you search for the ring, and lead and inspire others to do the same.

Some of you might be thinking, "But I'd be too uncomfortable to try anything like that." That's the point: *anytime you try something new that expands the boundaries of your comfort zone, you're going to feel uncomfortable, and that's okay.* In fact, it's better than okay. It's a sign that you are actually doing something different and trying out new behaviors. Often I tell my consulting clients who come to me for leadership coaching that if they truly want to change, they have to be willing to feel uncomfortable for a time. "If you call me up and say that you are feeling uneasy as you implement the changes in your leadership that we discussed, I'll say 'Good! You're making progress,'" I'll tell them. Someone once said that the only one who likes change is a wet baby, and I think that person may have been right. Many of us don't like change, and we fight it every chance we get. But if you can learn that you are not the center of the universe, that your way is not the only way, and if you are willing to step outside your comfort zone from time to time to try new behaviors and approaches to solving old problems, your ability to lead yourself and others through change will grow exponentially.

DIG A LITTLE DEEPER

1. *What kind of environment do you create for the people you work and live with? Is it fun and relaxed, or is it more serious and uptight? What would the people who work and live with you say? Ask them if you dare.*

2. *What can you do to nourish your sense of humor?*

3. *Are you comfortable poking fun at yourself? If not, why not?*

4. *Who are the leaders you respect the most, either currently or from history? How do they (or did they) use humor to their advantage? What can you learn from them?*

5. *Debate the following statement with a friend or colleague: "Humor has no place in the workplace." Practice arguing both sides.*

Chapter Seven

FINDING THE RING REQUIRES TEAMWORK: ENGAGING OTHERS TO DIG FOR THE RING

As my wife and I were experiencing this ordeal, we were amazed at how many people wanted to help out. There were phone calls and cards and letters, almost too many to keep up with. Even from people we didn't know. We were stunned by people's generosity and their willingness to do so much work on our behalf. What makes people want to give so freely of themselves in times such as these?

I t was clear to me that the CEO didn't get it. He was addressing the members of the sales group, trying to fire them up. He began by outlining his schedule for the last few years. With almost bizarre pride, he described sleeping in hotel rooms three out of every four nights. He detailed the deep sacrifices of his personal and family time that he had made. And then he made his Big Pitch, "Today, we are introducing a sales incentive program. If you put in the effort like I have the last few years, you have the potential to eventually make a million dollars!" He paused and waited for the enthusiastic uproar he was sure was coming. There was tepid applause instead.

Later, the CEO approached me backstage. "Gee, that really surprised me," he said. "I thought they'd go crazy when I announced that. Everyone wants to make a million dollars, don't they?" Uh, no. At least, not if it requires the incredible sacrifices he had apparently so willingly made. To be fair, I am sure that there were a few people in the audience who were jazzed by the offer. A million bucks was just the ring they were looking for, and they'd dig through any amount of rubble to get it. That was what mattered most to them.

Yet, judging from the audience's lukewarm reaction, the CEO had not inspired his sales group to dig as enthusiastically as he might have hoped. The CEO was a very bright man; nevertheless, he had made a cardinal and surprisingly common mistake of leaders attempting to motivate people to change: he assumed that what motivated him to dig for the ring would motivate them, too.

In my work, I have seen otherwise extremely talented senior leaders make this mistake time and again. They just don't understand that what motivates them won't necessarily motivate everybody else. And, they lack the insight to truly understand what makes people want to change. They focus on what *should* motivate people rather than on what actually does. I can't tell you how many times I've had frustrated leaders who are considering ways to motivate their workforce say, "I shouldn't have to motivate them. It's their job. We pay them a good wage to dig for the rings, so they should do it. I shouldn't have to hold their hand and place it on the shovel."

What these executives are missing is that people don't always do what they *should* do, but they always do what they *want* to do. Sometimes these actions are one and the same, but not always. Motivation is a psychological process, not a logical one. It follows from the laws of human nature.

All behavior can be viewed as an attempt to satisfy our needs, values, or beliefs. If you understand these aspects of a person, you can better understand that person's behavior. For example, if we have the physical need hunger, we eat. If we're tired, we sleep. Alternatively, if we have the psychological need to be liked, we act in ways that attempt to meet that need. If we value helping others, we may volunteer our time to serve the less fortunate. On the negative side, if we believe that our group is superior to others, we may behave in a prejudicial and judgmental manner toward those who don't belong.

The more you understand what motivates others, the more you can successfully lead them and engage them to dig for the ring. All you have to do is link digging for the ring with *their* strongest motivators, not yours, and people will dig with gusto. Failing to do this will result in frustration, wasted energy, and you wondering what went wrong.

One of my consulting clients had a raging internal debate among his company's management team. The company was to launch a new product that was key to its strategic and financial success over the next few quarters. The debate was over how to best motivate the sales staff to dig hard to reach this particular ring. The management team went round and round. One contingent was all for a tiered incentive program. With each milestone reached, the company would give the sales team some sort of bonus, culminating in an all-expenses-paid trip to the beach for all the team members and their families.

Another contingent felt that this was a much too elaborate and expensive approach. They argued that it would drain away too much profit from the project and would defeat the purpose of the incentive plan in the first place. The latter contingent bought into the "we pay them to sell, so they should just sell without any added incentive" rationale. Both sides dug in their heels, and they reached an impasse. Then they turned to me as their consultant.

"Gary, what do you think we should do?"

They had teed it up for me perfectly.

"You guys are trying to figure out how to motivate the sales staff, but you have left out one very important step."

"What's that?"

"Have any of you stopped to ask the sales force members what would motivate *them* to meet this particular goal? Or have you just assumed you already knew?"

Blank stares followed all around.

"I guess we just assumed we already knew what would motivate them," seemed to be the consensus answer to my question. "Or at least that's what we've been debating."

"My advice is simple," I said. "Why don't you go ask them what would motivate them to dig as hard as they possibly could in this instance?"

Before I tell you what happened, let me address the "they should do it because it's their job" mindset first. I know some of you are probably stuck on that. First, for those of you who hold this particular point of view, I agree with you to a point. People are paid to do a job, and they should do it to the best of their ability as much as possible. And, for the most part, I believe most people do. Most people will give you a good day's work for a good day's wages.

But, on a broader scale, people are motivated by far more than money. If you want them to reach down for a little extra, you had best figure out what would motivate them to do so.

Some of us are motivated to work hard because we like being part of a team; we like digging for rings together. Others are motivated by the sense of accomplishment and achievement we experience when we reach our goals. Maybe it's simply taking pride in a job well done, or feeling like you've climbed another rung up the corporate ladder or helped someone else do the same.

The point is, we're all motivated by something, but we're not all motivated by the *same* thing. It's your job as a leader to figure out what that thing is for a specific group at a particular time in order to achieve maximum motivation. Once you do, it's simple: hold out the carrot and get out of the way. Shovels are about to get busy, and rubble's about to fly!

If you're not sure what would motivate any particular individual or group to dig beyond what's expected, ask them. They'll answer you, either through their words or through their deeds. Or, as someone once explained it to me, if you want to know what someone is motivated to do, watch what that person *is* doing. If you don't see what you need, figure out what would motivate her to change. If you can't figure it out, then take the direct approach and ask.

Let's see how this plays out by returning to our story. In this case, the management team gathered the sales force together and explained the new product and its strategic importance for the company going forward. Further, management let the sales team know that it wanted to create a fun and energizing incentive that would keep the sales team loose, yet focused and motivated on moving this particular product, without breaking the bank. The members of the management team made no promises, but said they would like the sales group's input before rolling out and committing to the sales incentive plan for this project.

The people on the sales team responded as follows:

"When we hit the first sales milestone, everyone gets ice cream," they said. The members of the management team looked at one another.

"I think we can work with that," they answered. "What else?"

Reaching the next milestone would call for pizza for everyone, the sales force decided. Again management concurred. And so it continued until it came time to agree on the final incentive, assuming that all the goals were reached.

Management braced itself. This was the big one.

"If we hit all of our numbers," the sales force staff said, "you have to take all of us out to the local comedy club."

Management readily agreed. It certainly was cheaper and more doable than a trip to the beach, as was the entire plan that the sales force came up with compared to management's. The management team learned that the most important question to answer if you want to fully engage people in your effort is: *"What's in it for me?"*

Keep two things in mind: first, you shouldn't immediately assume that their answer to this question would be the same as yours, and second, the answer has to be something tangible and immediately relevant to them. It's not being thankful that one has a job or that the stockholders will benefit. You need to discover what's in it for the particular group in question. From a leadership perspective, if you take nothing else away from this book, take this: *if you want people to dig for the ring especially hard, you have to be able to answer the question "What's in it for me?" completely and honestly.*

If digging for rings will require some sacrifice on the part of the diggers, as it often does, you need to share that, too. They'll be smart enough to figure this out for themselves anyway, so if you don't acknowledge it, you will lose credibility. For example, it concerns me to hear executives tell employees after a round of layoffs that there will be no more layoffs down the road. How can management know that? Even if it's not in the plans, things change. Markets shift, products fail, the economy tanks, and another round of layoffs may become necessary. It's important to be as realistic and authentic as possible.

Employees know that layoffs happen, and when they hear management say something that flies in the face of common sense or their experience, they become unwilling to fully devote themselves and their energy to the needs of the business. They become distracted by trying to figure out whether management is keeping something from them intentionally, or whether the managers are simply in denial. Either way, such a stance does not engender confidence or do much to bolster morale.

As long as you tell people the truth and they can see what's in it for them, most will persevere and make the sacrifices you're asking of them. So another important leadership takeaway of this chapter is that if you want to keep the troops loyal and digging alongside you, always tell them the truth as you see it and know it now. Let them know that you will keep them informed as things change. They may not like what you have to say, but they will respect you for saying it. That's how you engender loyalty.

I once had some senior executives approach me with a gnarly problem. They had two top leaders in their operation. One was doing well, the other less so. In fact, they had decided to fire the latter. The problem? The two executives in question were married. The company's executives were afraid that if they fired the poor-performing spouse, the high-performing spouse would quit. The question was how to fire the one spouse without losing the other. "Have you been giving the poor performer feedback along the way so that he could improve his performance?" I asked. "If so, then this action should not come as a surprise to either one of them, assuming that they have decent communication at home."

The answer was, not really. The executives had been walking on tiptoe so as not to offend either party. That was their first mistake. I encouraged them not to repeat it. If they weren't going to give the poor performer another chance, then they would have to be up front about the decision and explain their reasons why.

Then, I encouraged them to go to the other executive and discuss their plans for her spouse and why (within the bounds of privacy laws), and share that they did not want to lose her at the same time. Keep in mind that it may now be too late. Holding back the truth at the outset is what got the executives into trouble initially. But they would compound their error if they repeated it, and nothing would be solved. Coming clean was their only viable option.

Engaging others to dig for rings with you is a fundamental leadership challenge. To meet that challenge
successfully, always be honest with people about what's
in it for them if they dig for the ring, both the good and
the bad. If they sense that you know what you're talking
about and you're being straight with them, they'll willingly follow you into the rubble with shovels blazing.

DIG A LITTLE DEEPER

1. *Think of a time when someone in management or position of authority told you something that turned out not to be true. How did that make you feel? What do you wish that person had done differently?*

2. *Think of a change you are leading other people through. What's in it for them if they go through this change? Have you communicated this to them? If not, why not?*

3. *What sacrifices will people have to make while digging for this particular ring? Have you acknowledged those sacrifices, while also highlighting what's in it for them if they do make those sacrifices? If not, what's holding you back?*

4. *Besides money, what motivates you to dig for the ring? What do you think motivates others to dig besides money?*

5. *If you're not sure what motivates the people you live and work with, how can you find out?*

Chapter Eight

What to Do When the Rubble Is Deep, Your Patience Is Short, and the Odds Are Long

The doctors finally came out after several hours and gave me the summary of where we were. The only possible way to save my son's life was surgery, but he was too little and weak to attempt it now. He would have to live long enough to gain the size and strength needed to survive the procedure; unfortunately, this was complicated by the fact that his blood vessels were shutting down, creating a lack of oxygen throughout his system. They said we could try an experimental drug that might buy us some time by opening his blood vessels, or we could do nothing and wait and see what happened. But, the medicine could also kill him by lowering his blood pressure too much. There was no way to know which way it would go, and I had to make the call.

My brother, Jeff, was in the process of buying a new home, and, as usual, the contractor had left paint and caulk and gunk in and on every room, bathtub, and window throughout the entire house. A few days before closing, Jeff found a solitary woman toiling to clean up the formidable mess. He was overwhelmed just thinking about what lay ahead.

"Do you mean to tell me that you're cleaning the whole house by yourself?" he asked her incredulously. "No," she replied blithely, "I'm only cleaning the room I'm in." This woman clearly had developed a strategy for dealing with what I call our Everyday Rubble.

Everyday Rubble accumulates from all of the small yet typical disruptions in our perfectly planned days. Traffic jams, cancelled flights, unexpected meetings, client crises, bulging workloads beyond the norm, unexpected days with no babysitter—all sorts of things can contribute to our pile of Everyday Rubble. Added to that pile are the larger and more ponderous chunks of rubble created by major changes in our lives, such as marriage, divorce, birth, death, job disruption, and the like. We can very quickly come to feel that we're facing a pile so high and so deep that finding anything of value within it is an impossible task. Ironically, some of us contribute to our stress level by needlessly adding more issues to the pile.

A story from one former colleague named Jim demonstrates this point.

One day Jim and his farmhand John were fixing the roof on Jim's barn. While they worked on the roof, Jim fretted about what else needed to be done. The fence needed mending, and he worried that they wouldn't get this task done in time for him to take his wife out to dinner; and what about the field that needed to be plowed? John finally put down his hammer, looked at Jim, and said, "Doc, why don't you just be doing what you're doing?"

"Huh?"

"Why don't you just be doing what you're doing?" John repeated, a little more forcefully.

"What do you mean?" Jim asked.

"I mean you're so worried about what you're *not* doing that you're doing a lousy job at what you *are* doing. You can't fix the roof *and* mend the fence *and* plow the field *and* take your wife out to dinner all at once! So why don't you just relax, focus, and fix the roof?" John summed up, picking up his hammer once again. "And stop driving me crazy!" he muttered under his breath.

Jim immediately recognized that John was right. He was creating his own pile of Everyday Rubble and needlessly adding to the stress of his day—and to John's—

and their performance as a team was suffering as a result.

We've all been there, needlessly adding to a stressful load that's already heavy enough by worrying about things that are outside of our immediate scope and control. John and the cleaning woman's rationale provides clues about how we might lower our stress level and achieve better results by not focusing on the entire stack of rubble that lies before us all at once, but instead addressing only the small piece right in front of us. Start with the pebble, not the boulder.

Once you've removed one small piece of rubble, focus on the next, and the next after that. Don't add to the pile by getting too far ahead of yourself (the What If sack) or constantly worrying about what's behind (the Resentments and Regrets sack). If you stay in the moment and remember some of the other techniques we've already discussed, the process will ultimately lead to the product.

This is also a wonderful approach to making change happen when standing still is no longer an option. Getting started is often half the battle—a battle that you'll win if you break down the task into doable chunks.

Recently we stayed at a warm and inviting country inn owned by a hard-working, middle-aged couple.

Their young children scampered about the lobby, adding to the family-friendly environment. It served to soothe the harried traveler's soul. Always curious, I asked the couple how they had come to own this wonderful little hotel in such a small town well off the beaten path.

Their story is a great example of how to find the ring by chipping away one chunk at a time at a seemingly overwhelming mound of rubble. It will inspire and instruct those of you who have dreamed of someday starting your own business, but haven't known where to begin because the task seems so daunting and distant as to be unattainable.

For years, this couple had shared the goal of starting their own business. The husband worked in the admissions office of a local college, and the wife was a mother and homemaker. They liked the small town where they lived, and they wanted to raise their kids there. They didn't want to move, but new business opportunities in that area were not readily apparent. That was their first chunk of rubble that they encountered—and a significant one. They removed it by doing some research, speaking with business professors at the college, and exploring resources online that would help them identify the types of opportunities and new businesses that would work in their area. It took some time, and they had to educate themselves along the way, but they kept at it. Finally, the couple settled on the idea of opening a small hotel akin to a bed and breakfast. The next obstacle was that they knew next to nothing about this line of work. Moving forward, the couple learned everything they could about hotels and hotel management. They went to seminars and conferences and visited other hotels, all the while maintaining their home and their current daily responsibilities. It took patience and perseverance, but they kept at it one step at a time. Eventually the two created a business plan for how it all might work. Next, they found a plot of land and drew up preliminary plans for the building itself.

The big boulder that remained was financing, typically the most resistant piece of rubble in most start-up scenarios. Again, they approached this impediment one chunk at a time. They spoke with several institutions, and after multiple rejections, they finally found a bank that was willing to work with them. Buying the land, building the hotel, and finally opening their doors to the public were the next chunks to tackle, which they did in patient succession. The day finally arrived, and they were in business at last. The entire process took several years, but they approached it one day and one chunk of rubble at a time.

Of course, every step of the way, they had to deal with unexpected changes and setbacks. And the Everyday Rubble was always there to deal with as well. But the two of them were focused on achieving their shared goal and avoided needlessly adding to their pile. And by clearing the rubble one piece at a time, they finally uncovered their ring, a beautiful hotel that my family and I thoroughly enjoyed.

Of course, life is all about change, and there was more rubble to come for this couple. Change doesn't stop once you find the ring. They still had the Everyday Rubble of managing a business and family life too, along with the more daunting rubble of market shifts, economic downturns, and keeping up with financial obligations. But they had come a long way from that couple who had a dream; they had made big changes through a series of small steps—digging through the rubble one chunk at a time.

I hope that by now, at least this much is clear: it's how we size up and assess the changes in our life, not the changes themselves, that makes all the difference in whether we are successful or not. Even when you are successful in finding the ring, there's always more rubble ahead. It's easy to become discouraged and start yearning for a simpler time with a straighter path to your goals, a path with fewer highs, lows, and ups and downs that accompany the rubble in your life. But life is all about those experiences. As the former *New York Times* columnist William Safire noted in his final regular column before he moved on to new professional challenges, "When you're through changing, you're through!"

Let me finish this lesson by sharing the inspiring story of a couple that was featured on the news recently—one that brings our metaphor of the ring in the rubble to life. The wife was doing some housework when she suddenly realized that her wedding ring was missing. A thorough search of the house led to one conclusion: the ring had gone out in the trash, and the trash had already been picked up and hauled away. Common sense said that the ring was gone, buried within the *42 tons* of rubbish at the local dump. There was no way the ring could be recovered, right? This husband and wife were determined to find it, and rather than give up, they started digging. In so doing, they put several of the tools we've discussed so far into use.

Invest time in people. *A friend knew the owner of the dump, who gave them permission to attempt the impossible by searching through the piles of rubbish for her ring.*

Invest time at home. *They dug for the ring together. It would have been easy for either or both of them to give* *up before they got started. By the time they were finished, both said that the process of digging for the ring together had brought them closer.*

You'll never find the ring if you don't start digging. *For two days, the couple and several friends dug through refuse that included deer carcasses, old tires, smelly sacks, and goodness knows what else. And as if the conditions weren't miserable enough, it rained.*

Engage others to dig with you. *The relationships and bonds that the couple had established with their friends motivated those friends to aid the pair in the endeavor.*

You're not the center of the universe. *They weren't afraid to look too foolish and weren't too proud to literally lower themselves into the rubbish in search of the ring. I have to believe that they kept their sense of humor about the situation and shared some laughs along the way.*

Break the task down into doable chunks. *Finally, a driver on a break suggested that they were digging in the wrong place and suggested that they begin chipping away in another part of the dump. Two hours later, miraculously, they discovered a bag of trash from their house. Moments later, they had their ring.*

When the rubble is deep, your patience is short, and the odds are long, you won't always find the ring. But if you pick up these tools and get digging, you'll give yourself a fighting chance.

DIG A LITTLE
DEEPER

1. *What seemingly impossible pile of rubble lies before you now? How does it make you feel?*

2. *Often, how you think determines how you feel. How can you change how you think about the rubble you face to make you feel more optimistic going forward?*

3. *What's one small rock that you can remove to get started, i.e., what's one small tangible step that will get you headed in the right direction? When will you take that step? Write it down.*

4. *Do you let the Everyday Rubble like traffic jams and such get you down? Can you accept that rubble like that will always be there and learn to let it go? What do you gain by holding on to these everyday minor frustrations?*

5. *Can you remember a time in your life when you faced long odds and beat them? Do you know of others who have done the same thing? What can you learn from those experiences that you can apply to the pile of rubble that you face today?*

Chapter Nine

THERE'S A FORTUNE IN FAILURE

If my son could survive long enough to gain the size and strength necessary for surgery, he'd have a shot. But it was a long shot at best. The planned surgery was very complicated, and they would be operating on a heart the size of a walnut. When the time came, we planned to take him to one of the best surgeons in the world, Dr. Al Pacifico at the University of Alabama at Birmingham.

I can only marvel at the skill and nerve of surgeons like Dr. Pacifico, who pioneered lifesaving techniques like the one he used on my son. Every time they step into the operating room, medical professionals face longs odds. The possibility of failure is high; when they fail, someone dies, and others lose a precious loved one.

We need to rethink how we view failure. Most of us see it as bad, as something to be avoided. Some of us believe in this perspective so strongly that they miss the golden opportunities because of an unwillingness to risk failure. The rings are there, but the shovel is in the shed. It used to drive me crazy in college when my friends were interested in a class but refused to sign up for it because they were afraid they could not get an A. Instead, they signed up for easier classes that they weren't interested in because they considered them safe. Who knows what rings of opportunity they passed up? Maybe sparks for a new career or the discovery of a passionate lifelong avocation were left buried in the rubble for fear of failure.

In business I see this phenomenon all the time. How many of us hold back from trying new things because we are afraid of how we will be perceived if we fail? We don't share ideas in meetings for fear of sounding stupid; we don't float that new product idea for fear it will be rejected; we won't even order new items on the menu at lunch for fear of being disappointed! That critical inner voice in our heads holds us back from trying anything new where failure is a possibility.

One of the wonderful things about children is that, for the most part, they don't labor under the burden of constant self-evaluation and apprehension and feel freer to try new things. I recall riding along with my six-year-old daughter as she drove a miniature race car at the amusement park for the first time. We jerked our way along, swinging wildly to and fro. I can still remember her head tilted back, hair flying, eyes closed, and face contorted with pure joy as she exclaimed with delight, "I guess I'm not as good at this as I thought!"

Kids don't consider failure a bad thing. They don't even interpret it as failure, and when we look at our kids, we don't see failure as a bad thing either. We recognize it as a tool for learning.

When our kid strikes out for the first time—fails a test, gets reprimanded for talking in class—we often say as part of the debriefing, "What can you *learn* from this?" With children, we recognize that failure is a tool for learning, and we rightly view it as preparation for success.

But if *we* dig for new rings and come up empty, our inner voice isn't so generous. *You screwed up! You failed.* In turn, we're more likely to give up digging all too quickly.

For adults, our ego is so tied up in being immediately and consistently perfect that attempting anything in which we might fail is incredibly uncomfortable. We passively stay on the sidelines, not willing to risk appearing foolish.

This in itself is foolish because almost nothing of value is created without the path to success being laden with obstacles and hard work. It took Thomas Edison thousands of tries before he perfected the light bulb.

The point is that if your initial attempts at finding the ring come up empty, keep at it. The ring is there; you just haven't found it yet. Use failure as a springboard to success, rather than as an excuse to give up. Here's a formula to help reshape your attitude toward failure: *Passion + Patience = Long-Term Success*. This should be your mantra whenever you find yourself in the middle of a long-term dig that, so far, has come up empty.

Passion means that you dig only for rings you care about. That's key. Patience means that you recognize that some digs will come up empty. It's to be expected. Rather than viewing empty digs as failures, consider them instead as stepping-stones to success. If you combine a passion for what you are doing with the patience to keep digging after inevitable setbacks, you will discover that there is a fortune in failure. The story that follows is a perfect example of this principle, and I hope it will inspire you to keep on digging when times are tough and the till is empty.

His life was hard. His father died when he was six years old, and his mother had to work two jobs to make ends meet. For several years, this youngster took care of his younger siblings, including cooking their meals. Adolescence treated him no more kindly. He fought with his stepfather and moved away, taking a job as a farm-hand at age 13. Later, he became a streetcar conductor. At 16, the young man joined the military, spending a year in Cuba. After his stint in the military, he returned home, married, and had three children. But even during adulthood, his string of misfortune continued. His life seemed to unravel through a series of failures.

The man had started a manufacturing company specializing in gas lamps. A trend toward rural electrification made his business obsolete almost before it began. He studied law through a correspondence course and became a lawyer, only to lose his practice after a violent outburst with a client in the courtroom. Finally he opened a gas station and added a small restaurant after customers asked where they could get a good bite to eat nearby. And there his luck seemed to change. This one-table, six-chair establishment grew to a 142-seat restaurant, complete with a motel and gas station. It seemed that he had finally found success; customers loved the simple, down-home meals he served. But when he tried to expand on his success by starting a chain of restaurants, the chain failed. Not to be deterred, the man moved to North Carolina and opened another restaurant and motel. That failed too.

Ultimately, he opened a motel that was successful—at least until gas rationing during World War II curtailed travel and forced him to shut down once again. Shortly thereafter, his marriage ended. Eventually, he remarried, this time choosing one of his employees. Professionally, he kept on digging.

The reopening of his business after the war became his greatest success to date. By the early 1950s, his restaurant business was worth $165,000, and he explored franchising both the restaurant and his popular recipes once again. It appeared that he had it made at last. Then the rubble of change struck again.

The government built a highway that bypassed his town and his restaurant. Once again, his business crashed. Eventually, he auctioned off his property for $75,000 to pay off his debts. By now, he was 66 years old and practically broke, living off his meager savings and skimpy social security checks. Every ring he had ever found eventually gave way to a new pile of rubble. What more could he do? All of his digs, despite his passion, had eventually turned up empty.

Reflect for a moment on all the setbacks this man endured. A lesser man would have given up, probably long before this. Few would have blamed him if he had. He had given it a good run, but things just didn't work out. Clearly, it was time to quit. But he refused. This man was still fueled by his passion for cooking and the recipes he had perfected over the years. And he had the patience to wait for whatever enduring success was to be his ultimate due.

Undaunted, he packed his beat-up car and traveled the country, sharing his recipes and cooking methods with all who would listen. The finer restaurants took a pass, but many "mom and pops" accepted his offer. They paid him five cents every time they prepared a dish using his methods. Four years after staring disaster down yet once again at age 66, he had 400 franchisees in the fold. Three years later he made $300,000 in profits before taxes, and one year after that he sold the business for *$2 million.*

His image remains the marketing face for the franchise to this day, and currently the business has more than 11,000 units in over 80 countries and territories. What's the answer? This man was Colonel Harland Sanders, founder of Kentucky Fried Chicken.

If frustrating change has thwarted your dreams, perhaps remembering this story will help you through difficult times or periods of insecurity. Sanders's series of failures served as a proving ground, preparing him for the success that was to follow—success born of his passion and patience. And what links the two is faith. Faith has two faces, one religious; the other is secular. Almost all religious faiths preach belief in a higher power. Calling on and relying on this higher power is a powerful way to endure the down times change sometimes brings. I encourage you to nourish, cherish, and lean on whatever religious faith may sustain you.

What I call secular faith is not a passive belief that everything will turn out okay in the end. It's an active belief that if you keep digging and trying without giving up, good things will happen. One way to keep the faith in dark times is to remember that sometimes today's rewards won't be apparent until tomorrow. The ring may lie just beneath your feet without you knowing it.

Practicing these two Ps does not ensure success. However, not practicing them almost guarantees failure. After all, a life devoid of passion is hardly a life at all. And if you don't practice patience, you're likely to flit from one thing to another, never stopping long enough to plant the seed that can thrive and turn into your life's passion. The act of digging for rings does not guarantee success. At times, perhaps many times, you'll come up empty. When you do, remember this bit of wisdom from

Henry Ford: "Failure is simply the opportunity to begin again, this time more intelligently." Most important, when you fail, it's what you do next that defines the line between winning and losing.

Losers give up and go home, condemned to a life of complacency and resignation. Winners keep digging with passion and sustain themselves with patience, a patience born of an active faith that better days lie ahead. I was perusing Monsanto's Web site recently and ran across a story that one of the company's employees shared about his father, a longtime farmer.

Early in life, I asked my father, "What would you do if you couldn't farm?"

He struggled with the answer and finally said,

"If I couldn't farm, I'd probably find some work, save a little money and try to get back into farming."

Farming isn't a job in my family—it's a mind-set, lifestyle, and tradition.

—MICHAEL DOANE,
AREA SALES MANAGER, MONSANTO

That's what it means to have both passion and patience, and this is the recipe for long-term success.

DIG A LITTLE DEEPER

1. *Can you think of a time when you tried to accomplish what you set out to do, but failed? What did you learn from that experience?*

2. *How can you apply learning from past failures to reducing your pile of rubble today?*

3. *When a toddler falls down, do we say that she made a mistake, or do we say that she's learning to walk? How can you change your thinking about your most recent dig that turned up empty?*

4. *Are you passionate about the ring you are digging for now? If not, can you envision a more attractive ring for you to pursue?*

5. *Think of someone from history or the world of business that you particularly admire and respect. How does this person handle failure? What is it about this person that inspires you? How can you apply this person's qualities or practices to your life when you might otherwise feel like giving up?*

Chapter Ten

The Secret Fears That Keep You Up Digging Well Past Midnight

I worried about what the quality of my son's life would be if he survived. I knew parents who cajoled and almost pushed their kids to be the best they can be. When you can visit your child in the neonatal intensive care unit for only 15 minutes at a time, four times a day, your plans for his bright future are in jeopardy. I remembered a colleague of mine who told me she thought nothing but Harvard or Yale would do for her son. Then her son was diagnosed with schizophrenia as a teenager. Once he reached his early twenties, his mother said that if he could keep even a menial job for more than a few weeks, she was just as proud as she would have been had he not been sick and was in an Ivy League school.

It never ceases to amaze me how many of the executives I know appear successful externally, but internally are a mess. And I'm referring to those at the highest levels of an organization. It seems that the more they achieve, the more distressed or anxious they become. These professionals sit in the power seat and are universally admired for their work ethic and success. Some are kind, others more cutthroat, but all are respected for their skills and accomplishments. Few people would imagine the inner torment that some of these individuals feel.

Fewer still could understand it. After all, these leaders seem to have all of the rings anyone could possibly want. Money, position, power, and prestige are all theirs. What more could they aspire to? They drive the best cars, they live in the biggest houses, and their kids go to the most prestigious schools. Outwardly, their lives seem perfect. But inwardly, they aren't. There's an undertone of misery that may be barely perceptible, even to them. But from time to time the nagging, relentless truth comes crashing through: no matter what they have or what they accomplish, it is never enough.

For these people, uncovering one ring in the rubble leads to an obsessive focus on finding the next. They rarely take the time to savor the moment. Life is all about digging through this pile of rubble to get to the next, and the next, and the next. And this is a recipe for burnout. Outwardly, such folks may appear confident, even cocky. And most of the time they feel this way inwardly, too. But sometimes, maybe in the still of the night, in the early hours when they wake up and their minds aren't consumed with constant activity, the thoughts and feelings they work so hard to hide creep through. Feelings of unworthiness and ineptitude—as if that person in the power seat is some kind of imposter. Such thoughts are terrifying. The need to quash them is intense. They feel the best way to do so is to get busy, to pick up a shovel and get digging. Because maybe when such people find that next ring—get that promotion, earn that bonus, make that sale, or deliver that product—maybe then, they'll finally feel like they've made it, and they'll find the peace and contentment they seek. That's the hope, but it rarely turns out that way.

My wife, Peggy, is a leadership coach for senior executives. She told me about one executive she met who stood out from all the rest. He was attending a leadership program and emerged as a leader among his peers. All the other attendees at the program looked up to him and took their cues on how to behave from him. Peggy said that this guy was the total package. He was tall, handsome, and smart. His interpersonal skills were excellent. He was a husband and father and the head of a business that was doing quite well. Many months after the program, Peggy was shocked to hear that this man had committed suicide. She learned that he had left a note, but she did not know what it said. But she did learn that the man had left an ominous sign—on top of the note was a mask.

I can't pretend to know why this man, who in most of our eyes had it all, would choose to take his life. But it at least seems clear that his outer appearance did not match his internal experience. The mask suggests that he didn't see himself as the man that other people thought he was. And who he truly was, we'll never know. But I do know that for some of us, this man's angst is not totally unfamiliar. We too carry demons that no one else sees or knows about. Thankfully, most of us never reach such a point of desperation that we attempt to take our own lives.

Nevertheless, life is not as fulfilling as we might like, despite our outer trappings of success. In this situation, all the rings in the world won't give us the inner peace we seek. Finding the ring becomes an internal battle for our heart and mind. That's a battle you can wage and win. Here's how.

I won't bore you with psychological theory, but rather let me get right to the crux of the matter: for a variety of reasons, when we're growing up, many of us develop self-beliefs that we aren't quite good enough. Maybe we aren't smart enough, strong enough, or likable or lovable enough. Perhaps we believe that we are lazy, physically unattractive, or just plain incompetent. Somehow, someway, we just don't measure up to the level that we (and others) believe we should. These negative self-perceptions come from all sorts of life experiences, not just from poor parenting, contrary to popular notions. Perhaps you compared yourself to a sibling and decided that you could never be as good as that sibling in your own eyes or in the estimation of others. Maybe your parents got divorced, and as a child you somehow got the idea that it was your fault. Or maybe you were the little one that all the bigger kids liked to pick on out on the playground or in the classroom.

Regardless of how they came into being, these negative self-thoughts became a part of your psyche, and you have had to live with them ever since. We come to believe the lie. They lead to one of the biggest social fears most of us will ever face: the fear of rejection. No one wants to think and feel that he or she isn't good enough and risk rejection from his or her chosen peer groups and loved ones. So, we learn at an early age to engage in behaviors that are designed to keep these negative self-perceptions and emotions at bay. To counter fears of being stupid, for example, maybe we study hard and become "smarter" than everybody else. To offset the belief that we are not likable or lovable enough, maybe we develop a "pleaser personality," always worrying about and striving to make other people happy.

Whatever the fearful self-belief is, we tend to do its opposite, and in spades. It's an unconscious process, but in this way we keep the negative beliefs and feelings under wraps, as well as our fears that the group won't accept us. The good news is, to some degree it works. Often, our compensatory behaviors drive us to do many of the things that ultimately bring us great success: we work hard, in fact pleasing teachers and later bosses, and we keep on digging for rings of opportunity long after others have given up. Rather than rejecting us, others reward us for such behaviors. Our family and friends praise us for our accomplishments. At work, we get promotions, raises, and opportunities to assume greater responsibilities. This feels good, so we repeat the behavior, which results in similar outcomes. The cycle feeds on itself, and the negative internal beliefs become buried under an avalanche of external signs of success.

But the downside of this dynamic remains: if you truly believe those negative self-thoughts, no matter what you do to quell them, it won't be enough. No amount of money, achievement, or accolades can keep them suppressed permanently. And if you don't maintain the behavior, the realization that you aren't good enough and the possibility of rejection are just around the corner. So you become like a duck heading upstream; you may look calm on the surface, but underneath you're paddling like hell.

In the end, however, no matter how many rings you accumulate, no matter how many degrees you have after your name, no matter how many rungs you climb up the organizational ladder, it's never enough. All this leads to a new and counterintuitive fear: the fear of success. In the previous chapter, we discussed how the fear of failure sometimes keeps us from digging for the ring. In this chapter, I want to emphasize that the fear of success can keep us digging too much, well past the point of positive returns. This is digging past midnight, and it's a problem that some of the most successful among us face. When we *have* to succeed in order to feel good about ourselves, success becomes like a drug: it results in a temporary high, perhaps in the form of gaining others' approval and enjoying the money, accolades, and internal sense of fulfillment that follow. But, as with drugs and alcohol, any high we experience from our success is fleeting. The sense of accomplishment and self-satisfaction fades all too quickly.

I'm not suggesting that *all* success is driven by our hidden insecurities—just that this is often the case. And when it is, it can be a terribly taxing and frustrating experience. No matter what we do, no matter how many rings we uncover, it's never enough to bring us lasting joy and fulfillment. So what can you do if you find yourself in this boat with others who have to "dig well past midnight" just to keep their anxieties at bay? What can you do to pursue the ring of success and still enjoy it when you find it, and not have its pursuit overtake all other aspects of your life?

First, if you recognize this pattern of *having* to succeed in yourself, good. Now that you see it, you can do something about it. Second, recognize that this pattern is quite common; especially among those we consider to be the most successful in our society. So you're in good company. Third, seize on this as an opportunity to reprogram the way you think about yourself. Many of us fall into the trap of defining ourselves by external measures: by what we have, what we do, or what others think of us. Our sense of self is dependent on external measures beyond our control. Recognizing this mindset in yourself is an opportunity for you to redefine yourself by a measure you can control. It's a chance to separate your sense of self and self-worth from the external rings of success that you pursue.

The goal is to move away from rings that you feel you *have to* pursue and begin searching for rings that you *want to* pursue. *Having* to succeed versus *choosing* to succeed is a subtle but powerful difference. The former is driven by feelings of inadequacy tied to mostly unconscious beliefs carried over from childhood. The latter is fueled by a more reasoned approach chosen consciously by you as a mature adult. So rather than run off antiquated thinking from your childhood, reprogram your mind based on your years of experience and accumulated wisdom.

Visualize and mentally decide how you choose to be now. I once had an executive tell me that for years he had scratched and clawed his way up the corporate ladder. He believed that he *had* to become a CEO, and he could not stop digging until he got there. It became an obsession. Then he became aware of what this nonstop digging was doing to him and those he loved and cared about. He was worn out—physically, emotionally, and spiritually. At home, he was losing touch with his friends and family. At work, his single-minded and self-absorbed approach was turning off coworkers and colleagues. Fewer and fewer people wanted to work with him, much less for him. As a result, his career ground to a halt. Ironically, he was trying so hard to become a CEO that he was sabotaging his chances of ever becoming one. Once he became aware of this self-destructive pattern, he reassessed his goals in life and how he was choosing to reach them. He finally decided that the cost of digging to become a CEO was not worth it. He abandoned this ring and focused his energy and efforts on the people and piles of rubble that lay before him right now, rather than looking ahead to the next challenge.

In short, he learned to reprogram his definition of success, and in so doing, he reprogrammed the way he viewed himself. Just as was discussed in Chapter 2, he learned to let go of the rings that he *had* to have so that he could latch on to the rings that he *wanted* to have in his life. And having reached this balance, he's been receiving promotions ever since. Freed of the burden of having to dig for rings, he relaxed and allowed the rings to come to him naturally, through a balanced portfolio of hard work and investing time in people (including himself). He stopped taking himself so seriously and broadened his focus beyond his narrow self-interests. His superiors noticed his newfound attitude and approach and rewarded him for it. And for him, success became something to enjoy, rather than a burden of increased expectations to be endured. Most importantly, he no longer made his self-worth dependent on external factors. As long as he was doing his job to the best of his ability and enjoying his family, that was enough for him.

Moving from *I have to* toward *I want to* is a process similar to what golf instructors preach: the easier you swing, the further the ball will go. So it is with success: the less you try to force it, the easier it will come. And the more you can enjoy it once it does. So if you are someone who *has* to dig for the ring well past midnight, it's time to relax and try a different tack.

Following the methods in this chapter and those covered throughout this book will point you in the right direction.

DIG A LITTLE DEEPER

1. When you were growing up, what lessons did you learn from your parents (or from whomever raised you) about what it means to be successful? How do you define success now?

2. How do those lessons and the beliefs you formed then play out in your life today?

3. How might you reframe your beliefs about success at this point in your life to get better results?

4. Do you define yourself by your external signs of success or by more internal measures? What are those internal measures? Do they motivate you or threaten you?

5. Try switching from "I have to" to "I choose to" when making choices big and small, both at work and home. See if you notice a difference in how it makes you feel.

Chapter Eleven

MOVING FROM PAIN TO GAIN WHEN THINGS CHANGE

My son was born six weeks premature, three days before Christmas. "Oh, this is awful," my mother moaned after she grasped all that was happening. "This has to be the worst Christmas of your life." At first, I had felt that way too. But over the last several days, I had had opportunities to stop and think about not only the pain of my situation, but also the gain. I had a child, my very first child, and I'd never had a child to love before. He was truly a blessing and the best Christmas gift I had ever received. I couldn't control whether he lived or died, but I could control what I thought, felt, and did. I decided I was going to focus on loving him for as long as I had him, and to let go of everything else as best I could. "No, mom," I finally replied. "I'm beginning to think this is the best Christmas I've ever had. I've never had a little boy to love before."

S pencer Johnson, the author of *Who Moved My Cheese?*, encouraged me to ask my audiences, "When people get fired, what do they almost always say six to twelve months after the fact?" The answer usually came back as Spencer predicted. "It was the best thing that ever happened to me!" people would shout out in unison. And it's true; many people who lose their jobs turn this into an opportunity to find a better one. Or, given the time to step back and reflect on what they want to do with the rest of their lives, they decide to make a career change, perhaps even start their own business. Many comment that the period between jobs turned out to be a godsend in terms of spending more time with their families and friends.

What started out as a dreadful experience often ended up being a positive one for many people who have been through it. That's not to imply that losing a job is ever easy. In fact, it can be painful and frightening on many levels. The initial shock, the possibility of financial hardships, and the blow to one's ego and self-confidence don't make it a pleasant experience by any means. It is to say that golden rings of opportunities lie in every pile of rubble, even though they may not be readily apparent. In the end, many people who for whatever reason lost their jobs feel that they ultimately gained from the experience. They feel this way because they learned how to deal with the pain of difficult and unexpected change to get to the gain. In this chapter, I'll show how you can learn to do this too.

There are three basic ways you can respond to the pain of change: ignore it and pretend it doesn't exist, wallow in it and make it seem worse than it really is, or deal with it and move on to something more positive. Let's explore each option.

In some instances, being able to ignore pain and pretend it doesn't exist can be quite helpful. For example, most athletes could not compete in their respective sports without blocking out physical pain to some degree. So, too, it's okay and advisable to learn to ignore the minor emotional pains, the frustrations, and setbacks that inevitably occur as we dig in pursuit of our goals. For these minor annoyances, it's best to notice them briefly and let them go. Shining your flashlight of awareness continuously on them only makes them seem bigger than they really are.

But smart athletes know when to heed serious physical pain and do something about it, lest they injure themselves more seriously. Likewise, when change brings serious emotional pain in the form of fear, anger, anxiety, sadness, or grief that feel overwhelming, we'd best do something about it too. Because as we discovered in Chapter 2, ignoring such emotions and bottling them up for an extended period of time is not usually, if ever, a healthy thing to do.

I once had an executive in a leadership development program who came into it livid. To hear him tell it, his company had been bought out by a bunch of idiots of questionable moral judgment who were now running the firm into the ground. As a member of senior management, he did not know how much more he could take; he said he was so upset that he might even have to retire early. For the next several days of the program, he attended a self-awareness workshop designed to help executives gain insight into the thoughts and feelings that drive their behavior. Afterwards, you could see that the man had been moved.

"My adult daughter died in a car wreck five years ago," he shared, as he began to talk about his workshop experience with the rest of the group. "Over the last few days, I realized that I had never truly mourned her death. At the time it happened, I did the 'dad' thing; I took care of funeral arrangements, saw to her estate, and took care of other people and their emotional needs. But I never got around to taking care of mine. I stayed strong; I don't think I ever cried about it even once. I was so busy taking care of everyone and everything that I never went through a grieving process."

He paused, and then continued in a quiet, emotional voice, "These last few days, I said good-bye to my daughter. I mourned her death. I let her go. It was one of the toughest things I've ever done. I don't like to cry, but I cried a lot these last few days. I thought I might never stop. But I did. And the funny thing is, now that I've gotten some of that out of my system, a lot of the anger I had toward work has gone away too. I mean, I still disagree with what those guys are doing, but I'm not nearly as upset about it as I was. I certainly don't need to retire over the situation. I want to stay and fight for what I believe."

Initially ignoring his pain from this most difficult change in his life had caused it to spill over into other aspects of this man's life, particularly at work. Finally being able to work through the pain allowed him to begin moving on. The bottled-up pain no longer clouded his view of everything else.

The second option for handling the pain of change is to wallow in it, an equally ineffective strategy. People who choose this option act as if they have blinders on. They tend to see and experience their pain to the exclusion of anything else. It's almost as if they wear their pain as a badge of honor. They have a hard time moving beyond it. There are some executives whom I call "self-awareness groupies." They participated in almost every leadership program that the firm where I worked offered, even attending some of the programs several times. They loved to talk about how much they got out of their learning experiences and how it all helped them become a better person and a better leader.

But to me, it seemed just the opposite. These people almost *never* changed. They came into every program and rehashed the same issues over and over. They became fixated on their pain and what it had done to them. Rather than use any insights gained as springboards for moving forward, they seemed to cling to these insights as excuses for staying put. In short, they talked a good game, but their performance was lame. They confused wallowing in pain with doing something about it. Hence, they never got to the ring of success they supposedly sought.

If you recognize yourself here, try throttling back a bit. By all means get professional help if you need it but don't spend a lifetime in therapy. Set goals with your therapist and work toward them. Perhaps the best way to overcome this tendency to become stuck in your own muck is to focus on helping other people. Reach out as a mentor at work. Volunteer at your local soup kitchen. Tutor kids. You'll focus less on your own troubles by helping others with theirs.

Our third option, acknowledging pain, letting it go, and moving on, is the best course, but often the most difficult. Ultimately it's the best path to finding the ring, but, like the executive who lost his daughter, we may have to work at it. Some of us are self-aware by nature and are able to express our emotions with relative ease and comfort. For many more of us, however, that's not the case. Men in particular often have a hard time acknowledging and expressing emotions, especially fear and sadness. We learn at an early age to "suck it up." For men, and for some women too, acknowledging pain and moving on requires time and effort.

Several years ago, one of my best friends was diagnosed with terminal brain cancer. He happened to be my boss and my mentor, and our spouses were quite close. For me, this was the most devastating change I had experienced to date. Over the next two years, I slowly lost someone whom I respected deeply and had come to love even more. But like many men, I found that allowing myself to grieve—to cry and to feel his gradual decline in the depths of my soul—was a very hard thing to do. It was much easier for me to stay busy and to try to help him and his wife whenever I could. Fixing things was my comfort zone, not feeling my pain. But I knew that if I didn't deal with the pain, in a very real way, it would come back to haunt me later. So I worked at it, spending quiet time alone where I could acknowledge my feelings. Ultimately this process helped me to say good-bye to my boss, and one of my closest and dearest friends.

It's important to create a way that will allow you to get in touch with your pain so that you can get through it and move on. For the executive who lost his daughter, it was a self-awareness workshop. For me, it was grieving alone. What worked for us might not work for you. You may have to experiment with how to get in touch with your pain and ways to express it.

Typically, there is no one thing that will enable this self-awareness and catharsis. You'll probably need to use a variety of methods and techniques to get in touch with your pain and move beyond it. Sometimes counseling might be necessary. But finding something that works is crucial because if you resist experiencing your pain, it will persist. And if it does, you'll miss out on the potential gains that change has created for you.

Think of this as a Pain/Gain Continuum. Imagine it as a line marked off in units from 1 to 100, where 1 through

20 represents Pain, 80 through 100 represents Gain and the numbers in between represent the journey from Pain to Gain. Now imagine looking at the line through your limited worldview. People who wallow in pain see only the Pain end of the continuum. Those who ignore pain see only the Gain side of things. They live in a Pollyanna world. Focusing on either extreme will keep you from changing, from finding the ring in the rubble. A broader perspective allows you to acknowledge the full spectrum of change and your emotional reaction to it. This awareness frees you to act, and to move away from the Pain toward the Gain. You see the rubble and dig your way through it to get at the ring.

Having the proper attitude is essential, too. I discovered this when working with outplaced executives. I learned that their attitude made all the difference in how they handled the situation they were in. A few were stuck in denial. They were sure that their former company would see the error of its ways and eventually hire them back. Others could see only the rubble and therefore stayed stuck in it. For weeks they complained about their former employer and the unfairness of it all. In both cases, these people's attendance at outplacement sessions was spotty, and their use of the resources available to them was limited. They didn't see the need.

Others started out understandably focused on the Pain end of the continuum and went through a period of mourning for their job loss. But they talked to their colleagues and maybe their outplacement counselors and did whatever they had to do to get through it. Then they got busy moving from the Pain end of the continuum toward the Gain. They took the attitude that finding a job had become their job. They got dressed every day and came to the outplacement center ready to work. Inevitably, they ended up finding better positions more quickly than their counterparts.

Early in his career, my brother went into work one day and was told that the company was shutting down that particular office. Everyone there was out of a job, including him. That afternoon, he went home in shock. He was surprised, hurt, and angry. But he didn't stay at that end of the continuum for long. He knew that feeling sorry for himself or complaining about what had happened would not pay the mortgage or take care of his family. So he put together his résumé and hit the street the following week. Three weeks later, he had a better job for better pay with a more respectable company in the same industry. He had taken a devastating change and turned it into a new career. Twenty years later, he's still with the company that hired him.

Similar examples spring to mind. When an executive I once knew was promoted, he discovered that his old boss from years ago (and longtime adversary) was now reporting to him. Initially, they both blanched and were stymied by the situation. Then they focused on the ring. They decided to use the situation as an opportunity to heal old wounds and improve their working relationship. I came in as a facilitator and helped them work things out.

Mergers represent another common example. Often business results fall short of expectations after a merger because leaders find it difficult to merge the companies' cultures. The acquiring company may force its way of doing business on the company being acquired, or at least that becomes the perception. Smart executives see the merger as an opportunity to blend the best of both worlds. They help people acknowledge the change and move beyond whatever pain the merger brought about by pointing out the opportunities to improve their work life and business results. When they do this, the company moves more quickly to the anticipated gains that the merger was designed to bring about.

Not everyone makes it in merger situations, of course. Some folks stay stuck at one end of the continuum or the other. Eventually some of them quit in bitter frustration or are let go. You can avoid a similar fate whenever unanticipated and difficult change hits you.

Remember: You can't always control the change that happens to you, but you can always control what you decide to do in response. Staying focused on the ring as you dig through the rubble is the best way I know to go about it.

DIG A LITTLE DEEPER

1. *When change happens to you, which end of the Pain/Gain Continuum do you tend to focus on?*

2. *What resources do you have available to help you express and work through your pain—friends, family, counselors, place of worship, and so on? List them all.*

3. *Are you using all of the resources available to you that you listed in question 2? How might you utilize them more going forward?*

4. *What's one tangible step you will take in the next 24 hours that will help you begin moving from the Pain end of the continuum toward the Gain end?*

5. *How can holding on to your pain in reality hold you back?*

Chapter Twelve

No Excuses:
Love What You Do
or Find Another
Place to Dig

During this ordeal Peggy and I experienced the gamut of medical care for our son, from outstanding service to egregious medical errors that nearly cost him his life. Most nurses, doctors, and technicians gave him unwavering professional, competent, and compassionate treatment, but a few others seemed to be going through the motions. The difference seemed to lie in their attitude toward their jobs. Most were passionately committed to quality patient care, but others seemed to be waiting out the weeks, months, and years until retirement. In this business, life and death hangs in the balance.

H ave you ever known folks who do nothing but complain about their jobs, but refuse to do anything about it? Don't they drive you crazy? If you ask them why they don't quit, request a transfer, or do something, anything else to improve the situation, they have a million excuses: I have a mortgage to pay; my spouse won't let me; I'm used to it; it probably wouldn't be any better anywhere else; my kid's getting married; my bills are too high; I don't have any other skills; this is what I know, and so on. Don't you just want to shake them? They act as if they have been dealt a bad hand in life and there is nothing they can do about it.

Their problem is not adapting to change that's already happened, it's how to make change happen when standing still is not an option—or, at least, shouldn't be an option. They haven't learned or accepted that if you don't like where you dig or what you're digging for, there are many other piles of rubble with buried rings out there for you to explore. This chapter is about how to make change happen when standing still is not an option. The key to it all is having a passion for what you do, and having the patience to wade through the rubble until you find the ring.

I remember, as an adolescent, watching my dad come home from work dripping with sweat. I thought,

That's going to be me someday. If I am going to come home looking like that, I sure hope I pick work that I enjoy. Happily, I've been able to live up to that childhood aspiration for the most part. I have learned that there is honor and satisfaction in all work, and that each job deserves to be done to the best of my ability. I have been a dishwasher, a shoe salesman, a gofer in an auto repair shop, a health insurance claims adjuster, a short-order cook, a deliveryman, a bowling alley worker, a sound-man for a rock 'n' roll band, a truck driver, a crisis intervention counselor in a hospital emergency room, a psychologist, a consultant, a speaker, and more.

In every job, I learned something. Sometimes I learned about myself, other times I learned about my coworkers, and in all cases I learned about human nature. I've had great bosses and horrible ones; cushy working conditions and crummy ones; good-paying jobs and poor-paying ones. Mostly, I've learned that it's not so much *what* you do for a living, it's *how* you go about it. You can go to work with a passion and a zest to do your best, ready to enjoy whatever the day may bring. Or you can go to work with a chip on your shoulder, miserable and determined to spread the pain. The choice is yours. We get stuck when we deny that we get to choose our work experience, when we think that external factors like lousy bosses or lazy coworkers determine our internal experience. That's when life looks like one big pile of immovable and impenetrable rubble.

I'm not trying to say that you should always go to work with a smile on your face or that every day and every job doesn't have its less appealing aspects. I am saying that, in general, if you don't enjoy what you do, and don't bring a positive attitude to it, then it's not worth it, no matter what your salary may be or how many other perks your job may provide. And, I'm saying you are in control of whether you like what you do or not. Ultimately, you get to decide when and where and how to dig, and how you go about it.

Here's a case in point. Six years ago, Paul was a city cop and Julie was a restaurant hostess and shift manager. Today they own a big house across from me that puts mine to shame. They are the nicest young couple you could ever want to meet. Here is their story.

Although they were happy back then, Paul and Julie dreamed of owning their own business someday. They loved ice cream and had done some research on opening a franchise, but they had not yet found anything that suited them. One day Julie was summoned to a table full of customers at the restaurant where she worked. Instead of the complaint she expected, they informed her that they were talent scouts for the television show *Wheel of Fortune*. She had a great, outgoing personality, they said. Would she like to be a contestant? Six weeks later, she and Paul boarded a plane for the West Coast. Little did they know the fortune they were about to uncover, and that it had nothing to do with the show (although she ended up doing quite well on that, too).

During their travels, they discovered an ice cream shop called Cold Stone Creamery. After several visits and much research, they decided that this was the opportunity they had been looking for. Once they got back home, they took a risk, took out a loan, and opened only the second Cold Stone Creamery franchise ever on the East Coast at the time, and the first ever in North Carolina.

I first met them as their customer. They worked like dogs. One or both of them was always in the store, no matter what time of day or night I went, and all the while Paul kept his job as a police officer. But they clearly enjoyed what they were doing. Their enjoyment rubbed off on staff and customers alike. It was always fun to go to their store; they made buying ice cream an experience. And it didn't hurt that the product was great.

A year and a half later, Paul and Julie took another big risk. Seeing the potential of the franchise, they took out another loan and opened a second store. More importantly, they also bought the rights to develop all other Cold Stone Creamery franchises that might open up in North Carolina in the future. Smart move. Their first store was the ninety-ninth one in the chain. Today, the chain has over 3,000 stores. More than 30 of those stores are in North Carolina. Paul and his partners recently bought the rights to develop all the stores in South Carolina, too. This young couple has become a tremendous success any way you look at it. The lessons come from examining how they did it.

It all started by following their passions. There are hundreds, if not thousands, of franchising opportunities out there. One reason Paul and Julie chose ice cream was because ice cream was something they both enjoyed together. This may seem like a minor point, but I would argue that it isn't. Perhaps they would have been just as successful opening, say, a chicken or burger franchise, but I doubt it. Their success clearly flowed from a love of what they were doing, and they were doing what they love. That was evident when you visited their store, and it is evident today when they talk about their dreams for their future. It wasn't hard for them to bring a positive attitude to their work, because they loved what they were doing.

Second, they worked hard. They didn't buy the business as an investment and then expect someone else to run it. They were in the store every day, and they saw to it directly that things were done to their satisfaction. They gave their employees appropriate training, and their employees seemed to enjoy working there. There's a direct correlation between employees enjoying what they do and customers going to a store and enjoying themselves, too.

Finally, they have clearly enjoyed their journey thus far and are energized about their plans going forward. They are a young couple still, with two small children. If financial success were the only thing they were digging for, there wouldn't be much left for them to pursue. While I am sure they enjoy the financial rewards that their hard work has brought them, I can tell that for them, the joy is in the dig and not just in the rings it may produce. Paul and Julie's story contains one other essential element that was and remains key to their success: their willingness to take calculated risks.

Taking out the loan for their first store had to be an intimidating experience. Extending themselves further with their additional stores and buying the store development rights had to be scary as well. Here's the point: *Making change happen almost always involves incurring some level of risk. You will rarely find any rings of lasting value if you never risk anything in your pursuit of them.* And it is the very act of taking risks that can make it all worthwhile in the end, even if the risks don't turn out as you had hoped.

In Gail Sheehy's book *Pathfinders*, she asked people in their late eighties and nineties if, looking back, their life had been worthwhile in their eyes. I remember one man's response as being poignant, sad, and instructive. I'll paraphrase: "I can't tell you if my life has been worthwhile because, looking back, I don't feel as if I *lived* it."

When Sheehy asked him to explain what he meant, he continued, "I always toed the straight and narrow line in my life. I always did what I was supposed to do even if it didn't match what I wanted to do. I never took any risks in my life. And now you ask if my life has been worthwhile. I tell you, I feel as if I never lived it."

Again, I am not talking about going out and doing outrageous stuff. I am not endorsing taking risks that make no sense or have no inherent gain to them. I am encouraging you to consider that if you want to find a ring of any value, you have to risk something along the way. Here's a simple tool for risk assessment: when contemplating a risky move, ask yourself what is the worst *realistic* outcome possible should things go awry. If you could accept this outcome, go ahead. If not, perhaps the risk is too great and you should consider an alternative course.

Often it feels as if the biggest risk is the risk of failure and all that that implies. We talked about that in Chapter 9, and we discuss overcoming the fear of failure in more detail in Chapter 13. But for now, think about baseball players; they risk making an out every time they step up to the plate to bat. Consider further that the most successful baseball players fail to get a hit two-thirds of the time. They could refuse to fail by refusing to come out of the dugout. But as Teddy Roosevelt eloquently explained, it's *not trying* that represents the greatest failure of all:

It is not the critic who counts, not the one who points out how the strong man stumbled or how the doer of deeds might have done better. The credit belongs to the man who is actually in the arena, whose face is marred with sweat and dust and blood; who strives valiantly; who errs and comes short again and again; who knows the great enthusiasms, the great devotions, and spends himself in a worthy cause; who, if he wins, knows the triumph of high achievement; and who, if he fails, at least fails while daring greatly, so that his place shall never be with those cold and timid souls who know neither victory or defeat.

Or, in my more modest language, *the joy is in the dig.* A few years ago, I attended a speech given by Warren Bennis, one of the most respected authorities in the field of leadership development. He shared how he had come to go into the field in the first place.

As I remember, Dr. Bennis explained that he had been a very successful college president, so much so that he was asked to give talks and advice on how to be successful in that arena. After one of his talks, Dr. Bennis said, a question came floating up from the back of the room, a question that arrived like a kick in the stomach and ultimately changed the direction of his life.

The question was simple enough: "Dr. Bennis, do you *love* what you do?" The question stopped Dr. Bennis cold, because at that moment he realized that although he was good at being a college president and had lots to say on the subject that others found helpful and useful, in his heart and soul he didn't truly *love* it. And, if he didn't love it, was it something he wanted to continue doing for the rest of his professional life and career? Ultimately, his answer was no. Dr. Bennis made a change. He pursued his true love and passion: studying leaders and leadership and contributing to this field.

In this chapter I have stressed the importance of doing what you love, and that the joy is in the dig, not just in the rings that your dig may produce. So how can you discover your passions if you are not sure what they are? There are many ways to do this. For example, what aspects of your current job do you like most? Is it working with people? Not working with people? Is it the intellectual challenge? Is it the satisfaction of solving problems and being able to point to tangible results at the end of the day?

On this last point, for many executives, work becomes less satisfying the higher up the organizational ladder they go. That's because the higher you go in an organization, the less your job is to do something tangible and the more it is focused on concepts like strategy and future direction and people development and relationships with Wall Street. Some executives miss being able to point to something concrete and specific that they did at the end of the day. If that's the case, you may have to redefine what you find satisfying about work or find other ways to get those needs met.

If circumstances and common sense dictate that you stick with a job you don't necessarily love because it wouldn't be prudent to leave it for some reason, don't use that as an excuse to give up on pursuing your passions. Find a hobby or a volunteer position outside of work that draws on the capabilities and talents that get your creative juices flowing. Meanwhile, you can always begin working toward the day when you can better align your true passions with whatever it is you do to earn a paycheck.

If nothing comes to mind in this arena, seek out resources like books and career counselors that can stimulate your thought process and help you explore just what it is that you love to do and how you might go about doing it. Observe friends and family members who seem to love what they do and ask them how they discovered that love and got into that line of work. And once you figure out what that might be for yourself, don't hesitate to get started.

Having a dream and a passion isn't enough; you have to actually pick up the shovel and start digging if you want to find the ring. Remember the couple we discussed who opened their own hotel? It took several years, but they finally realized the passion of their dreams. It took the combination of passion plus patience for their dreams to be realized, just as it will for you. Don't settle for digging for anything less than what you are passionate about. Anything else simply isn't worth the effort.

DIG A LITTLE
DEEPER

1. *Do you know what you love to do? Do you have an HR department or a career counselor that you could approach to begin to figure it out?*

2. *How easy is it for you to get out of bed each day before you head off to work? What thoughts run through your head, and what do you feel as you head to work?*

3. *What can you change at your current job that would make it more attractive to you? Can you talk to your boss about taking on new roles and responsibilities? Can you transfer to another part of the operation? Can you sign up for new skills training?*

4. *What kind of person greets your family or friends when you walk in the door at the end of the day? Is it someone you would want to greet on a daily basis?*

5. *What reasonable risks are you willing to take in search of a better ring at work?*

Chapter Thirteen

But I'm Afraid: Pick Up the Shovel and Dig Anyhow

When our son was four months old, he weighed seven pounds. His heart problems and a cleft palate made eating very difficult. The surgery we had hoped to put off until he was older and stronger could not wait any longer. We had come to Birmingham, Alabama. Before the surgery, I was holding him in my arms, knowing that the orderlies were coming to take him to the operating room in 15 minutes. I knew that I might never see him again after that, and I began to panic. If this was all the time I had left with him, I didn't want to fritter it away consumed by fear. Instead, I focused on my love for him as best I could. Then the orderlies came and took him from my arms. They wheeled his gurney onto the elevator, The doors shut, and then they were gone.

Y ou can't talk about change without talking about fear. It goes with the territory. Unfortunately, fear is not an easy topic to discuss, especially for men. We adopt the attitude that "fear is for wimps." Many of us, men and women alike, much prefer to get angry than to feel afraid. Anger empowers us; it points to an enemy that we can rail against. Fear, on the other hand, makes us feel weak and passive. That's why you'll see some people become very angry and stay that way when things change. Anger is a good cover-up emotion; it hides from view softer emotions that we'd just as soon avoid. We get angry with management; we get angry with our boss. We blame politicians for our troubles, or perhaps we even blame God. We'd rather be draped in self-righteous anger than be overcome with crippling fear. But fear is a part of nearly every change we face and every change we hope to make, so we had best learn how to deal with it. In this chapter you will.

Einstein once said, "Insanity is doing the same thing over and over again and expecting a different result." True enough. I'm no Einstein, but I'd like to propose an updated and complementary version of his dictum: insanity is doing the same thing over and over again and expecting the *same* result. As we have explored throughout the book, change is constant. Today's plans are tomorrow's pile of rubble. Technology becomes obsolete almost before you can implement it. Markets shift, consumer demand is becoming more exacting, and fulfillment demands are accelerated. Competitors become more aggressive.

The scary thing is that the path to winning in this environment is rarely very clear. You have to forge ahead with no guarantee that you are on the right path. And then, just when you are making headway, change comes along, and you're confronted with another damn pile of rubble. We find ourselves longing for the way things were. In fact, if you look hard enough, you'll realize that those good old days weren't so different from today.

Especially since the beginning of the Industrial Revolution in the mid-1800s, we have been on the fast track to the discovery and innovation of new and exciting ways to do business, travel, communicate, and so on. It only seems that the times we are in now are moving more rapidly than ever. The truth is, it's been that way for at least a couple of hundred years (and, in reality, for much longer than that).

The most successful businesses and trade associations are always experimenting with new ways to dig. Rather than bemoan the changes in their industry, they are embracing them. In fact, they are going beyond just embracing change; they are creating it. It's true that some of us are more wired from birth to embrace and create such change. Others of us are more wired to find comfort in the status quo. And all of us are wired to fear things that can physically harm us. But most of us fear so much more than that: rejection, looking foolish, being wrong, and appearing stupid. Those are the fears surrounding change that we can overcome. Because each of us, regardless of our original wiring, can learn to shake off the cobwebs, face our fears, and contribute by digging for new ways of doing business and new ways to create value for our markets, our organizations, and ourselves.

I learned this lesson the hard way. Once I completed my graduate work, I landed a job working for a leadership-consulting firm that hired psychologists. It was a dream job: the work was interesting and challenging, I liked my coworkers, and it tapped into my personal and professional strengths as best I could determine them. Over time, however, almost imperceptibly, my dream job turned into a nightmare. I shared with you earlier that my boss and mentor was diagnosed with brain cancer a year after I joined the firm. His slow decline and eventual death were personally devastating, but they had professional implications, too.

This was a small firm, and Nate was a key player. Trying to compensate for his gradual departure was taxing for all of us, including him. Collectively we were a tight-knit group, but the stress strained all of our professional relationships. When Nate finally passed away, we all carried on as best we could, but it was clear that the firm that I had joined was now no more. Over time, I became increasingly unhappy, frustrated, and angry. I focused my anger on the owner of the firm, who had reinstated himself as the day-to-day leader following Nate's death. Jim was a great man and a great teacher, but his mercurial nature made him very hard for me to work for at times. I became increasingly convinced that he was the source of most of my problems at work.

I was hiding behind a veil of anger. Some of my anger was a cover for my grief, although I do think that I did a good job of working through that grief overall. Mostly, my anger was a mask for my sadness at the realization that things had changed; I had lost what had been a very special place to work. Now what I had was just a job, and one that I did not like very much. What had happened wasn't anyone's fault, especially not Jim's. Eventually I figured that out. He had the right to run his business however he saw fit. I had the right and the responsibility to figure out whether I could stay there and support him in my role as one of his managers.

I finally decided that I could not. It was time for me to leave. There was only one problem: I had a fat, new mortgage at home and two young children to take care of. It wasn't the best time to be considering a job shift, especially since I had no immediate prospects at the time. So I did what any mature, self-respecting professional adult would do: I went in to work one day and quit. I hadn't planned on doing it, at least not then. I had thought about it, but I had not reached any conclusions until that day, when it just seemed to be the right time and the right move.

At least, it seemed that way until I started driving home. Talk about fear. I began to imagine what was going to happen once I walked in that door.

"Honey, guess what happened at work today? . . ."

"YOU DID WHAT?!?"

That's pretty much the way it played out. I am lucky that Peggy didn't leave me on the spot, and I couldn't have blamed her if she had. But she stuck with me, and I did my best to reassure her that everything would be okay. After all, we had $15,000 in the bank and time to decide what to do next. At least, we did until I did my taxes right about then and realized that I had made another big mistake. Our $15,000 nest egg was now down to $7,500 because of my miscalculations on what we owed that year. Up until then I had been feeling strong and confident about the change, but now I wasn't so sure. Fear rushed in. However, Peggy and I forged ahead with starting our own business, as we had decided to do after a round of heart to hearts. Somehow, we made it.

What I learned about fear as I went through this process and others like it over the course of my early years is that fear is not a bad thing. It is God and nature's way of protecting us from harm when something threatens our physical survival. Without fear, we simply wouldn't last very long. However, real problems occur when we react to non-life-threatening events as if they were life-threatening. Jim used to say that it would be like the military setting its missile detection radar to go off every time a butterfly flew through. Some of us set our "change radar" in much the same way. Whenever things change, our minds immediately jump to the worst possible scenario, and we react emotionally as if that scenario has already occurred. There are several ways to combat this tendency.

First, stay in the moment. For example, I shared with you that I started to panic when I was holding my son in my arms and realized that they would be coming to take him into life-threatening surgery within 15 minutes. But I quickly realized that if I spent the next 15 minutes worried about what *was going to happen*, I would miss *what was happening* right then. I refocused on loving my son for whatever time we had left together. The situation didn't change, but I changed the way I saw it; therefore, my experience changed.

Much of our fear of change is self-induced. Like we saw in Chapter 2, we play a game of What If: What if the economy turns and I lose my job? What if the housing market crashes and we can't sell our house? What if my retirement fund goes bust? All of these are reasonable questions and concerns, but they are focused on future events that have not happened, and therefore they cannot harm us *now*. What Ifs are part of the baggage that will keep you from experiencing the importance of the moment. Unforeseen events do occur, so prudent planning for the possibilities is a smart thing to do. But here's the key: don't fear what's not real. Don't react emotionally as if there is an imminent threat to your survival when there is not. Plan for later, but live *now*.

I recall a woman I met who said that she was always in fear of losing her job. She worked in a struggling industry, and she constantly worried that her company would be sold, that it would fold, or that she otherwise would be downsized out of her position. Her concerns were legitimate, but her fears were crippling her rather than enabling her. She learned to overcome this tendency by recognizing (1) that she had a job *now* and there was no *immediate* threat to her well-being, and (2) that rather than worrying about the potential worst-case scenario, she could actively prepare for it. So every Sunday she looked through the classifieds for positions similar to her own, inside and outside of her industry. She noticed what skills and experience employers were looking for, and then she set out to improve her skills in those areas through taking classes, getting on-the-job training, and requesting relevant assignments. In doing this, she immunized herself against the negative effects of a change that hadn't happened yet but potentially could at any time. Meanwhile, she did her best to stay in the moment and enjoy what she had rather than worry about losing it later. She planned for the future but lived for today; she turned her worries into action. She turned her fear of change into a rational plan. This didn't totally eradicate her fear of losing her job, but made it much more tolerable. She was prepared, come what may.

It's important to understand that fear is never going away, nor should we want it to. It's wired into our DNA, and it's there for our protection. The key is to control your fear rather than letting it control you. As we saw in the last chapter, one way to do this is to consider the most *realistic* worst-case scenario should your fears become reality. Can you accept this as a possibility? Could you live with it if it happened, even though you wouldn't like it? If so, don't let the possibility of that scenario stop you from making the changes you want to make. On the other hand, if the most realistic worst-case scenario is something that you imagine would be too much for you to handle, then perhaps you should listen to your fears and try another tack.

Digging for rings can be risky business. Every time we set out to make change happen, we run the risk of failure. But if we let unrealistic fears stop us from making the attempt in the first place, then we have failed before we ever began. If you want to find the ring in the rubble, realistically assess your fears. If they are protecting you from imminent harm, heed them. If they are not, be afraid, but dig anyhow.

DIG A LITTLE DEEPER

1. *What do you know you want to do career-wise, but are afraid to do?*

2. *What is the realistic worst-case scenario if you tried to do this and failed? Are you willing to accept that outcome?*

3. *Do you let fears of what others might think stop you from doing what you really want to do (assuming that what you want to do would not harm others)? If so, are you willing to be afraid and do it anyhow?*

4. *If you stay on the career path you are on now, how will you feel when you look back and take stock at the end of your life? Will you take pride in the choices you made?*

5. *If fear is stopping you from doing what you want to do, is that fear protecting you from real dangers or imaginary ones?*

Chapter Fourteen

Rings Don't Come Free; Make Sure the Price You Pay Is Worth It

They always say that something like this causes you to reorder your priorities in life. I've discovered that that's true. My daily worries and concerns over whether my son lived or died put everything else into perspective. None of us knows how much time we have left on this earth. And yet, often we seem content to allow our time to be consumed by trivial matters, when we are capable of thinking and doing so much more. I was not naïve enough to think that I would come out of this experience a perfectly balanced person who would no longer let life's traffic jams send me into a tizzy. I liked to think, however, that when I did revert to treating meaningless setbacks as if they were true impediments to my happiness or success, I'd recognize my mistake more readily and move on.

Everything comes with a price. That dictum applies to pursuing the ring of opportunity, too. Make sure the ring is worth the price you pay for it. I once heard a senior executive say that he owned two homes, and that he had spent exactly 30 nights in each during the past year. The rest of the time he was traveling for business. He said it was the price he paid for success.

We are an instant gratification society. We want what we want, and we want it now. As consumers, we demand a lot of our service providers, and if they don't meet or exceed our expectations, we go somewhere else. That is all well and good. The problem is that we adopt that attitude in all aspects of our lives. If someone isn't working out on the job, rather than give him honest, tough-love feedback, we ignore the problem until we are forced to either let him go or shuttle him off to Siberia until he finally decides to quit on his own. If we diet, we want to lose 10 pounds *now*, not wait for several weeks. All of this behavior has a price.

Ironically, in a book that's all about learning to love and embrace change, I want to leave you with this final message: it's okay to take your time. You don't have to try to change overnight, nor should you. It's okay to fail and to try again. It's okay to stay in a bad situation and try to work it out or try to make it better. I'm not saying that if something is not working for you—an employee, a marketing plan, a product launch, a personal relationship—you should just sit back and accept the idea that that's the way it is. I am saying that sometimes we are too quick to change, too quick to jump to the "next big thing" without realizing that we already had the next big thing in our grasp, but we let it go because of our impatience. Too many businesses follow the pack to the latest fad without deeply asking and examining "Is this the right path for us?"

In fact, the best leaders rarely chase after fads. They realize that just because popular notions would seem to indicate that something is "the thing to do right now," that doesn't necessarily make it the thing to do right now *for them*. Organizations whose leaders don't understand this pay a heavy price for chasing the popular ring of the moment rather than pursuing rings that make more sense in the long run.

Have you known or worked for organizations that get caught up in the cost-cutting waves that periodically hit their respective industries? They almost blindly let people go without considering the longer-term consequences of losing so much intellectual capital and experience at once. Inevitably, they end up shorthanded. The people who remain are overwhelmed, having too much to do and not enough time or expertise to do it. Sometimes the offending companies have to rehire the folks they recently let go, either as full-time employees or as consultants. It's not that controlling costs doesn't make sense. It's that doing it because everyone else is, doing it outside the parameters of a larger strategic plan and approach, or doing it solely to silence the wolves on Wall Street, that almost always makes it a bad idea in the long run.

When change reduces your plans to rubble, digging for the ring of opportunity is the thing to do. But if you are bored, or out of ideas, or simply getting lazy, then take a long, hard look in the mirror. Rather than go looking for new rings, maybe it's time to shine and polish the treasures already in your possession.

Early in my career, I met two very wealthy men who were in their early thirties. They owned a business together. They had met each other in their late teens, when they worked together as laborers in that very business's warehouse. Over the years they had worked their way up until they were able to buy the business. Each of them was married; they drove fancy, expensive cars and lived in sprawling mansions. One of them owned property at the beach. They were the very pictures of the American dream. They had worked their way up from

the bottom to the top. There was only one problem: neither was very happy, at least as compared to their earlier years, as they reported to me.

They let me listen in on their conversation one day.
They were reminiscing about the early days, when they
had had very little money and had just gotten married.
They talked about going crabbing together on a
Saturday morning, then hooking up with their spouses
that afternoon for a beer and crab fest. They compared
that to their current circumstances, where their spouses
were isolated in their respective mansions, trying to
manage a support staff of gardeners, cooks, and the
like who could never seem to get things quite right. The
two friends rarely saw each other outside of the office,
as they now had so many commitments related to their
wealth, such as managing their property at the beach.
They concluded that while they were thankful for their
material success, it had come at a price. Whether that
price was too high only they could say. Similarly, only
you can determine what price you are willing to pay
for whatever golden rings of opportunity you choose
to pursue.

The moral of the story is to go ahead and chase
the golden ring at work. It's fun, vital, and necessary in
today's business world to keep up the chase. Just make

sure the chase makes sense in the long run, for you and for your organization. And chase the golden ring at home. Never lose sight of life's other treasures, and make sure that when you finally get the prize you seek, it does not turn out to be fool's gold in the end.

DIG A LITTLE
DEEPER

1. *What types of rings does your organization tend to pursue: the fashion of the month, or something with a little more long-term value?*

2. *What price does your organization pay to chase these rings? Are they worth it?*

3. *Individually, what price have you paid to pursue the rings of your dreams? Have these rings been worth it?*

4. *When it comes right down to it, what rings matter most to you in life? What are you doing to pursue those rings right now?*

5. *How will you know if the rings you pursue are actually fool's gold, rewards that ultimately won't be worth the price you paid to achieve them? And, what will you do about it if they are?*

Epilogue

My son had open-heart surgery at the age of four months, when he weighed seven pounds. He survived. We took him home, and three weeks later he went into congestive heart failure. We had to send him back to Alabama by air ambulance, where he underwent emergency open-heart surgery. He then weighed six pounds. He survived. Then they discovered that he had another hole in his heart that had not been apparent before. They told us that if he did not gain weight, they would have to go in a third time. He remained in the hospital and slowly gained weight, a gram at a time, or about a paper clip's worth every 24 hours, over the next several weeks. We averted a third surgery, but just barely.

Then he wouldn't eat, probably because of all of the tubes that had been put down his throat. He would gag if a crumb hit his tongue. We had to feed him via a pump and a tube inserted into his stomach. He needed surgery to put tubes into his ears. Twice, while he was hospitalized, he was given overdoses of medication that nearly killed him. Over the next two years, he had hernia surgery and surgery to close the cleft palate in the roof of his mouth.

This little guy endured more in his first few years than anyone should have to in a lifetime.

But I quickly learned not to complain. Other sick babies were much worse off than he was; some didn't make it. At least I still had a child to cherish, love, and worry about.

Finally, at the age of two, he started to take food by mouth, and eventually we were able to remove the tube. Gradually, he grew and gained strength. Today, as I write this, he is a relatively healthy, totally normal, pain in the butt teenager whom I love with all my heart and soul.

He still has a hole in his heart, and we still have to go in for periodic checkups. But if I have learned anything from all this, it's this: there truly is a ring in the rubble, and there is treasure in every trouble.

Here's why. There was no way I could see it then, but his tough start in life and battling through it has become an inspiration for people all over the world. I share his story whenever I speak, and people tell me afterward that it lifts them up.

While I would never choose to go through that experience again, much of what I have shared with you in this book about how to find the opportunity in change I began to learn from him, both from how he survived the ordeal and from the experiences that Peggy and I endured together.

His start in life and subsequent battle taught me, like nothing else has, that we can't always control what happens to us, but we can always control how we choose to respond. That insight, and the peace it has given me over the years, as well as the confidence to persevere despite whatever odds I might face, has been one of the greatest rings I've ever uncovered.

I have been pleased to share my son's story and tools for finding the ring with you. I hope you have picked up practical tips and will be inspired to do great things, and find great fortunes, whenever things change for you, as they inevitably must.

When change happens, will you complain and hesitate, or will you start digging? The choice, you see, is yours.

ABOUT THE AUTHOR

Gary Bradt is one of today's most popular speakers on the leadership circuit, addressing corporate audiences around the world. His clients include IBM, General Motors, American Express, General Electric, eBay, FedEx, and NASA. Bradt was endorsed by Spencer Johnson as the leading speaker worldwide on Johnson's business bestseller *Who Moved My Cheese?*

His Web site is www.garybradt.com.